A Spider's History of Love

MIRCEA CĂRTĂRESCU

A Spider's History of Love

Translated from Romanian by
Adam J. Sorkin
and

Radu Surdulescu • Daniel Mangu • Ileana Ciocârlie • Ioana Ieronim
Mirela Surdulescu • Cristina Hanganu-Bresch • Bogdan Ștefănescu

POEMS COPYRIGHT © 2020 by Mircea Cărtărescu
TRANSLATION COPYRIGHT © 2020 by Adam J. Sorkin
COVER AND BOOK DESIGN by Alexandru Oprescu

All right reserved. Published by New Meridian, part of the non-profit organization New Meridian Arts, 2020.

No part of this publication may be reproduced, or stored in a retrieval system, or transmitted in any form or by any means, electronic, mechanical, photocopying, recording, or otherwise, without written perimission of the publisher, except in the case of brief quotations in reviews. For information regarding permission, write to newmeridianarts1@gmail.com.

LIBRARY OF CONGRESS CATALOGING-IN-PUBLICATION DATA
A Spider's History of Love
Authored by Mircea Cărtărescu

ISBN: 978-1-7343835-2-2
LCCN: 2020941783

Contents

Once I Had...

Love Poem \ 3
Let's Make Love \ 8
So Long! in Bucharest \ 11
Mechanical Toy \ 12
You Owned All Sorts of Electrical Devices \ 14
History of an Ocean \ 15
Not a Thing About Survival Technique \ 18
Our Love Has Gone... \ 19
Memory of an October Evening in 1984 \ 21
Self-Portrait in the Flame of a Lighter \ 24
Woman, Woman, Woman... \ 27
Sonnet ["be careful when you step between tramcars..."] \ 34
Sonnet ["it seems you're made of cellophane, it seems you can be won at dice"] \ 35
Sonnet ["then all at once you start to wonder"] \ 36

Bebop Baby

Bebop Baby ('Cause Tonight You'll Be Mine) \ 39
A Motorcycle Parked Beneath the Stars \ 43
Gypsy Queen \ 45
I'd Like to Be Your Friend \ 46
Little Elegy \ 48
The Beast \ 50
Skeeter \ 52
I'm Smiling \ 53
Adriana \ 54
Beer and Cold \ 56
Do You Know the Country Where Lemon Trees Bloom? \ 59
A Vodka at the Caraiman Bar \ 61
I'm Given a Copy of "Howl" Signed by Ginsberg \ 63

The Girl with Socks of Diamond \ 68
Letter with Armpits \ 70
Call Me, Call Me Today at Last! \ 72
My Life's Getting Crowded \ 74
Eye to Eye \ 76
You Always Astound Me \ 78
A Crown of Thorns \ 79
Mircea Cărtărescu in the Fall of '87 \ 81

Prisoner of Myself

How It Is \ 88
Clouds Over the Building Across the Street \ 90
I Beg You \ 92
Sábato Would Have Taken It for an Omen \ 94
Women \ 96
Oh, Natalie… \ 99
The Scent of Dry Leaves \ 102
A Very Good Poem, with Satanic Sadness and a Montgolfier of Despair \ 104
Once I Had Visions, Now I Have… \ 106
I'm Jealous, Damn It… \ 108
Winter Sunlight \ 110
I Walk down Water Lily Street in the Bright Sun \ 112
A Sudden Autumn, August 30, 1989 \ 114
The Occident \ 116
August 14 (Listening to "Woman") \ 122
Nothing \ 123

Mircea Cărtărescu \ 125
The Translators \ 126

Acknowledgments

THE TRANSLATORS ARE GRATEFUL to the editors and publishers of the following magazines and books in which poems in this collection previously appeared:

the literary magazines, *Another Chicago Magazine, Apostrof, Calende, Connotation Press, Cutthroat, Exquisite Corpse, Glint, International Poetry Review, Lana Turner, Metamorphoses, Modern Poetry in Translation, New Delta Review, Parthenon West Review, Ping-Pong, Poem* [UK], *Poetry New York, Poetry Wales, Ramuri, Respiro, Romanian Civilization, Saranac Review, Talisman*;

the chapbook, *Bebop Baby* by Mircea Cărtărescu, *Poetry New York* Poetry Pamphlet Series No. 19 (New York: Meeting Eyes Bindery/PNY, 1999); and

the anthologies, *Leading Contemporary Poets: An International Anthology*, ed. Dasha Čulić Nisula (Kalamazoo: Poetry International, 1997); *Romania and Western Civilization / România și civilizația occidentală*, ed. Kurt W. Treptow (Iași, Romania: The Center for Romanian Studies, 1997); *Day After Night: Twenty Romanian Poets for the Twenty-First Century*, ed. Gabriel Stănescu and Adam J. Sorkin (Norcross: Criterion Publishing, 1999); *Speaking the Silence: Prose Poets of Contemporary Romania*, ed. and tr. Adam J. Sorkin and Bogdan Ștefănescu (Pitești, Romania: Editura Paralela 45, 2001); *Born in Utopia: An Anthology of Modern and Contemporary Romanian Poetry*, ed. Carmen Firan and Paul Doru Mugur with Edward Foster (Jersey City: Talisman House, 2006); and *Bucharest Tales: A Collection of Central European Contemporary Writing*, ed. John a'Beckett (Warsaw, Poland: New European Writers, 2011), rpt. Contemporary Literature Press, ed. Lidia Vianu (Bucharest, Romania: University of Bucharest, 2014).

Warm thanks to Mircea Cărtărescu, who approved the publication of his poems in the translations in this book.

*THE TRANSLATORS OF EACH POEM ARE INDICATED BY
INITIALS IN BRACKETS BELOW THE LAST LINE OF THE POEM.*

Once I Had...

Love Poem

    a stuttering lunar eclipse sputtered gobbledygook on TV
    that Sunday when, caught as if in a neon tube, you were commiserating
            with me,
    we were commiserating and grinning, meowing, swaddling ourselves in
            Chinese cherry wine, we were trading small talk
    as I nibbled at your pendants, your image in mirrors, your neck
    and then if you remember we were going to make crepes and through the
            kitchen window the Dîmbovița Mill
    kept clattering its paper rolls of rat-free ghosts
    the factory chimney was made of real bricks, nothing was metaphysical
            and that excited you
    as you let your breasts glow in the winter dusk
    like the light globes of our childhood classroom humming above the
            school supplies
    nothing metaphysical, just high-pitched nerves, a kind of screech of
            purple cellophane
    in sublingual corridors
    just a way of pressing your finger across two poorly insulated wires
    and in the demented kitchen you showed yourself bright and translucent
            like a two hundred thousand carat jewel
    and deep down in the digestive tract I could spy
    death herself.

    I saw her leaning against the iron fence of the TB hospital next to the
            police headquarters
    stopping a kid on the sidewalk to send him to fetch a newspaper or a fresh bun
    and I saw her shopping for bread and newspapers in the pinkest, most
            incomparable sunset

I saw her poor and decrepit, reaching out filthy paws in stained white
            crocheted gloves
to grab the bar on the front door of the trolleybus
imploring with a strident Negro voice, hitching her skirts up, facing the
            glassy stare of the living and breathing foxes
that nipped at the driver, and in her stomach generations of yogurt lorded
            it over cookies candies Turkish delight
I saw her belly on an inflatable pillow galloping across the steppe of her
            sequined bikini
with her lungs inhaling a tincture mixed from liquid silver, the down of
            oneiric visions and lamé
in the mystical dive of the Orient bar, and, behold, it was the hour of
            the hashishins
and as she danced shining with the effect of blue light in your heart and
            cartilage and marrow
I saw her gossiping over a cognac, speaking into a microphone, chatting
            away during the time of dinner and bed and guitar,
of hemispheres and ice caps, talking,
talking and talking and talking about Marcuse, about Antonioni, about
            Stratan, about dyes and grammars, ultimately
always talking about the same hypertrophied labyrinth
I saw unnatural death, death fabricated from synthetics
and death that flares like an oil rig on fire
emptying her subconscious full of earwigs and bisulphate in gasps
over universities and statues and garlands of athenaeums and lakes
melting Enescu's statue in front of the opera house, making it into
            giant mousetraps
hidden under the chairs of the Tosca Café
and I saw her languorous black body swallowing the north-south highway
            and seeping into the ground
dangling like a sinful spider from the network of sewers,

I saw death in a sailor suit, a monkey
watching me from the third deck with sad red eyes
her peduncles hanging from the undeveloped encephalon of a chimpanzee,
I saw her delousing her rubies in the region between liver and pancreas
I saw her carrying refrigerators and curling her tongue to lick stamps and
        attaching several written pages with a wire paperclip
yawning without covering her mouth before sublime sunrises with the
        stench of aphrodisiac and bromide
she was the methylene blue they scraped my conscience with, incognito
        under tonsils and polyps
and I recognized her in the idiotic design on matchboxes…
paralogical beauty, I once knew a lot of jokes
and my mother sewed the lining of my pockets out of her pre-war and
        pre-marriage memories
I let her round, sharpened hands perform complicated open-skull
        brain surgery
and a much more complicated decoupage of my heart.
then winter came, yet long before the passageway in the center of the city
        was built
people gathered underground there as if lured by perfumed prophesies
and crowds of foreigners hovered in the air with lit cigarettes where now
        the intercontinental hotel has its terrace
and embryonic kittens groped in the steam vented to the streets
        by patisseries
was I complicated? oh, bacteria visited me like going to a store or a museum
the skin over my skull muttered the semantic aura of a weary usurper
and my ears were tuned to squeals of inward ecstasy
conjoined with the apocalyptic hullabaloo of boulevards lined with cinemas
sullen beauty, the night's garter belt unloosed in sleepwalkers an
        orchestration of fetishisms
the child I used to be pokes his head out of my thorax

his bangs draping the armchairs and floor lamp in a brilliantine slipcover
bodiless and barefoot he sneaks into the bathroom
smears the mirror with rosy aftershave
and squeezes toothpaste into the porcelain toilet bowl
he looks into my eyes his cerebral hemispheres fluttering silently,
       so very well-behaved.

love, amour, eroticism… Bauhaus design sipped like daiquiris in
       champagne flutes
blood-red with smeary lipstick traces
that's what they call heritage and we should descend into Mateiu
       Caragiale's heraldic dementia
and Pișcu's universe. but I suppose you prefer clonic movements
and a grand hysterical crisis
you prefer that countless dresses and feelings be molded to your breasts
and that no one should miss your mesmeric countenance with their
       watery, superannuated eyes
that someone should release himself from the aldehyde of the
       improbable, the improbable in the twilight
and carry you in his arms to orgasm like a medusa in which humors and
       reflexes float
that someone should embrace you unawares putting you at ease
then place a mirror before your beautiful face
so you can admire yourself, in dream, with a smile's trace…
so you can see yourself as little girl and young lady and whore and mother
       and Electra and buxom housewife and matron and virgin
lymphatic, melancholic and choleric and immutable, sanguine—
death,
grinning a big grin….

the lunar eclipse stuttered so badly that the screen exploded burying us
        under a rainbow of windshield glass
the Dîmbovița Mill fell to ruin its stone blocks like a flooded city beneath
        the Atlantic
the winter twilight outside gestured desperately, its hands over its long fur
        coat beating its back
and pointing to the first star, vegetal, cherubic…
nothing metaphysical: in the courtyard, dump trucks were cooing, then
        inside us, our intestines
trimmed the Christmas tree with little electric stars
oh, that oilcloth eyes could converse with your brassiere
you yourself could throw spitballs of purple cellophane into the
        catacombs under my tongue
we can love one another, adore one another, make love, sleep together
touch each other with a cold conscience, bite each other's cheeks
with lacy teeth
transplant into neon and nothingness a death made of spongy diamond
a two hundred thousand carat death.

        [A.J.S./C.H.-B.]

Let's Make Love

let's make love, *ma cher amio*, let's make love *toujours*
for tomorrow we'll be prey to floods, landslides, blind drunkenness,
for tomorrow a yesterday will creep on a hay spider's legs through the
        flowery curls of your hair
bewildering you, befuddling you....
let's be tender, mumbled the Cățelu Driver's-Test Course, irises fixated
on the voluptuous hips of the Filaret Bus Station
let's be tender, my loneliness, chirped the traffic-circle sign,
let's be tender, buzzed a fly.
the spring licked our faces like a Pekinese, licked our hands,
made us wonder how the infinite tongue of night teeming with buses and
        stars might taste,
the spring caressed us trespassing the bounds of motherliness or
        innocent friendship,
displaying her cold provocative breasts through a threadbare turquoise jacket.
oh, please stay, whispered the lampshade to the carpet's loose thread,
won't you come upstairs with me? we'll have a drink, listen to music,
I can show you the bookcase...
why don't you spend the night at my place?
let's hold hands, lisped the little tin rabbit in the toy store window
to an internist at the Emiliza Irza Hospital
let's make love, let's dally in amour, let's grow and multiply,
sang the velours, the moleskins, the tweeds and toiles on Gabroveni Street
and the cops on the beat and the puffy clouds would repeat this till they
        turned hoarse
let's do that thing, hissed the hair salons.

like light bulbs wired in series,
the nerves on the forearm kept firing, the veins on the thorax bulged,
the smell receptors in the nostrils hung their winter coats in closets
and the refractive index gorged on a chicken sandwich
in the perverted stare of the eye.
how many glances, how many careless accidents,
closed accounts, paid-up policies,
my little angel, sneezed the lung admiring itself in the mirror
and sizing up the factory behind it.
spring slathered a thick slice of TV on bread
our mind was clogged with aggressive projects, we'd already seen the
        microcosm riddled with trenches,
we'd already dreamt of power, of krakatit, of the smell of the invisible
        man's fox fur
and the velvety eyes of the man who walks through walls...
our brains remembered when they waited curled up in a ball
when they pulsed, when they throbbed, scurried, writhed, twitched,
        squirmed, wriggled,
the forearm thrust into the thin air had an impression of feathers,
the ear—an impression of tingling from a triceratops bellowing,
hydrogen bubbles slapping malaria's cheek.
believe in me, cooed the intestinal flora
stretching voluptuously in the arms of the horror
bedecked for the evening in a simple fitted suit, quite youthful,
give me a little kiss, anabolism coaxed catabolism,
don't be cruel, stop torturing me, grinned mandible to mandible.

evening fell, the city came to life,
night fell, the streets fizzed like soda-water.
let's be tender, losing lottery ticket, let's be tender, rug-beater,
let's make love, faucets, let's take a trip, writing-case!
in robes of rubbish and green wicker, of cold cuts and sliced cheese,
varnished with vodka and diesel, the emotions went tomcatting.
in dead-end alleys and passageways roofed with colored glass
a kitty would scratch at the wooden trestle of a laurel tree,
and in the beer joints waitresses would let themselves come unscrewed
        and fully alive for a fee.
let's make love, Unamuno, madman, let's make love, *ma cher amio*,
and then let's cheat on each other with the matchbox, the pliers,
        the toothpaste,
let's ignore the influence of the Grozăvești dorms
on our psyches.
spring stares yellow through the stratosphere, tickled by ozone and ions,
let's get to know each other better, snail, it proposes,
let's hug, depot, scrap of paper, dumpster…
and at the fountain at the end of Alexandru Alley we'd squirt one another
right beside the clinic, where even the trees
smelled like a dentist's.

                                              [A.J.S./C.H.-B.]

So Long! in Bucharest

once we were so close
that I'd remember episodes from your childhood
and dream your dreams
when you ate your rainbow at the ice-cream parlor next to Scala
my face kept changing colors…
once we were so happy
that in college we'd both share the same desk
and the foundation on your forehead seemed
more important for humanity
than all the great geographic discoveries.
we'd go for a walk, under the TV-colored umbrella dissolving
the shops in the passageway with frappes, teddies, and quacks
your five-foot-one
swept the asphalt before us
and the bright beam tore through the dark of the boulevard
outside the Very Small Theater
and bore into your memory other voices, other rooms…
but it's over, it's over! from now on, along with what lovers
will you stumble under the stars, under boulders of diamond?
now the frost of time has almost silvered
the ice rink of your frosted hair.
so long!
so long!
so long!
good-bye, dear love, in this autumn!
from now on our amour will trench the asphalt for sewer pipes
to assure a decent quality of life.
there's one thing more I want to tell you—
last night the Romarta Department Store
collapsed from loneliness.

[A.J.S./C.H.-B.]

Mechanical Toy

this fall there were leaves of gold on the trees
and they fell with a crunch on the curved macadam
this fall women wore a miniature gold Pekinese
activated by a complicated mechanism

the wind itself flickered from tiny transparent gears ever wheeling
women all had feelings
the houses were spongy with square balconies
everything was rolling *r*'s with a grin, stretching chewing-gum breasts
everything depended on the Pekinese with a catch
operated by a complicated mechanism

"love me, love me!"
"squeeze me, squeeze me!"
this fall I have a gold myocardium and every doctor wears a surgical gown
the operating rooms are crinkly cellophane
"take care of me"
"I'm feeling down"
my life was difficult, controlled by a cogged gear and rod
step by step I tiptoed along the curved macadam
"love me!" the women, the Woman, She, cried out in a spasm
motivated by a complicated mechanism

the wind polished its jewel, its dial, its crystal face
I listened to the gold leaves scatter with a crunch
on the macadam
and to the Pekinese with their crass insolence clicking their nails of strass
on the macadam
oh, and the trolleybuses were stuck in an impasse…

"why don't you want me? why didn't you want me? where does your resistance come from? your insistence to decide by yourself what we should both decide together? why don't you write me? why didn't you send me a cassette with the sound of your voice? whom have you turned into? what happened to the memories we shared? where are our friends?
in what bed
are you baring your true body?"
"love me!
squeeze me!
care for me!
stretch this fall like chewing gum
look at the ripped dresses in the store windows
watch gold leaf peel from your skin, your cheeks
look: a ray is passing through the apartment buildings of ruby bricks"
the gear-toothed wind goes whirring by
and gold leaves fall with a crunch on the curved macadam
activated by a key of gold, by springs of gold
by levers of gold, by flywheels of gold
spinning, reversing, squeaking,
complicated,
complicated,
complicated…

[A.J.S./R.S.]

You Owned All Sorts of Electrical Devices

you're built differently from me. you freak me out.
you're a monster. I'm scared of you.
you've got things I don't. you've got breasts, for example,
you've got attitude.
you've got heaps of dresses, you've got relatives with university degrees,
and, my God, how your hair flows down to your knees
like a ghostly fruit truck that seems to hover
as it rolls softly along Dorobanți Boulevard.
and you've got hips, you've got tantrums, you've got lovers…

your subconscious must be so immense
that it alone could bridge every urban versus rural difference
and put an end to the wave of pornography and violence
with a simple gesture, or a salve.
why, if you were a documentary on the valences
of the chemical elements
and I were the sheet-metal of a silo roof
we still wouldn't be as opposite and aloof
as here in an actuality of athenaeums, cabernets, automobiles.

when you touch me I tremble, I'm nonplused by your voice on the phone.
why should there be a creature like you?
why now should there no longer be one?
you beast, freckled temptress, wanton,
cape thrown loosely over maxillae of tin,
silly goose.

[A.J.S./C.H.-B.]

History of an Ocean

upon the plate-glass windows of the Unirea Department Store,
        the evening deposited thin sheets of lapis lazuli
the parked cars seemed folded from tinfoil and smelled of patchouli
violet, depressive and empty, the north-south avenue pointed to the clouds
as after emotional disillusionment
when, suddenly, nothing happened to transpire
suddenly, everything was much like just before
child differed terribly from child, clothes from clothes, cigarettes from
        cigarettes, teeth from teeth
tire from tire.
because everything was in tears, in the evening everything shed cascading
        blue teardrops over six inches wide.
and the teardrops kept asking each other:
"do you love me?"
and
"well, do you love me?"
"how much longer will we stretch illusion on our skin, curved and bare?
and you, windshield, yes, you, shoe, who are you?
who are you, Cișmigiu Gardens, smoking like a blue snare,
what color is your life, Intercontinental Hotel of velvet?"
"little fly, what use in the world is your caviar?
cicada, spider, golden rhinoceros beetle, scorpion,
why are you alive, window, architect, waterfalls, spigot, peon?"
the drops were hiccuped, panted, sighed,
the houses became pink pig-snouts, elephant trunks, mandibles pinching
        the evening so convoluted and profound
the drops kept breaking free, flowing into the pedestrian
        passageway underground
blue wave after yellow wave after withered wave

and though everything was hallucinatorily the same as before,
the little muscle in the corner of your eyes also shed drops of greenish,
        hot tears,
they flickered on the latticework of the gutters, they asked in very loud voices:
"what are we? hurry up there, where's your IDs, bushes of opal!
hurry up, star cluster, strip for your mandatory physical!"
and likewise asked in very loud voices:
"are we hormones, cuffs, biorhythms, blunders, engines, sluices?"
and then your tear fused into the unanimous tear
which flooded the whole of life, the whole of the evening
under a vast, flattened teardrop, scintillating with iridescence,
gliding toward the passageway in innocence.
behind it remained no trace of scenery
behind it remained junked auto bodies twinkling ardently towards the celestial
and a kind of rabble with flesh winking like asphodels
with an eye socket a little splintered
with stiff gizzard.
they were a bit taller and more filiform than us
and asked themselves:
"will it fly, this airplane of pus?
will anybody touch our lips?
will we be as delicate as a button seen in the dressing table mirror
by the girl's lashes like blue and mauve arches?
will we ever come
to nibble on an atom?
will we hide there under the atomic rind,
        deep
                deeper
                        even deeper?"

"do you love us? do we love us? do you love me?
do we love?"
and they stared at the teardrop, shrunken and glossy,
flowing down all the escalators at once into the passageway.

God, how your skirt hung stiff and shredded into scraps while you were
        standing in front of the Unirea Department Store
and your skin crumbled into pieces like old paper
your flesh fell in crusty flakes like plaster
your skeleton disintegrated: the maxillae, phalanges, tarsi, vertebrae
dissolved into dust as after a fever
and of the store there remained a few steel uprights,
a handful of aluminum hangers, some haberdashery…

I'll go down into the passageway, among holothurians,
        gudgeons and coelenterates,
I'll knock with my fins on the plate-glass
I'll touch the shoals of parrot fish with lips stretched wide
here's the balloon fish, the lobster lurking where the pharmacy once was
the cuttlefish levitating above the counter for café-frappé
everything enveloped in such tranquility, such tranquility!
here's the hermit crab, the little crayfish with sea anemones on its back,
a classic example of symbiosis.

                                                        [A.J.S./R.S.]

Not a Thing About Survival Technique

compared to you, the constellations are a frump
the city lights are a dumb joke, dead on delivery,
the breezes in the air
sailing by you like liquid consignments
wolf down the birds and crush plant spores
between their teeth, spreading only the stench of rotten luck and guano
to new volcanic earths in Melanesia.
your femininity colors in my crises of *pavor nocturnus* with a demented hue
my memories of you in the Garden of the Icons Park, when you used to
        put on your makeup shamelessly
in the convex mirror of the Anglican Church or a setter
yes, our love was upping the district record another centimeter…
you, redemptress, tender confederacy of systems and apparatuses
who'd gamble his small allotment of precocity
on your pink and sinuous hierarchy
and who'd intuit your sweet duplicity
selvaged with snack bars and a Breughel of velvet
in this tangle of no one, nothing, nowhere, nevermore?

beyond everything, half-hearted moral beauty,
a brilliant diminishment
and the reality of discussions and mutterings over crystal cups
at the Negoiu Restaurant
beyond everything, that grumpy jubilation of the sole survivor
of an ocean liner of feelings.

[A.J.S./I.C.]

Our Love Has Gone...

'80-'81, what a winter!
a cloying swamp of coffees, cigarette lighters, "Dire Straits,"
        literary circles, glasses
and at night a quagmire of painful jelly: faces, calves and petty gossip
sometimes a glance out the window, at the traffic hardly making its way
        through the snow.
but here's the sun! has spring understood us at last?
the windows in the Obor Market are gleaming, and the Colentina
        Highway looks yellow
the asphalt stinks of tadpoles more seductively than ever, there are
        gasoline rainbows,
there are Albanian sardines in oil, and women and schoolgirls
stare contemptuously at the shop window with kitchen appliances.
farther on, the trees in the courtyards have burst forth into bud
the traffic signs now appear like folded newspapers
like doves of rust. yes, the powerful sun lighting up
all these factories, water towers, schools, the cemetery…

—and me? I'm playing my part in the general happiness.
here's how: I got off the 109 bus one stop early
and I devoted myself to mindless wandering in the grass along the
        highway's shoulder.
the dump trucks, the TIR international transports, the semis roaring back
        and forth
in their steel armor, carrying pipes, sacks, mortar
the trams gliding past as in dream…
such that I had to sit down on the curb and study the sparkling grass.
here, take a look, a bee defiled with dust
a cellophane candy wrapper

a beetle with a crushed elytron, fleeing lopsidedly, these things happen
at the root of a blade of grass, trembling
in the balmy breeze blowing out from the window of the wire factory.
a blue sky, the sun, shadows interwoven, engine-exhaust sounds
golden tram-rails, green grass blades, earthworms, beetles...
could Tao and Bodhisattva have yearned for more?

The Hill was rising up softly with pillars, houses, limousines, the highway,
            I no longer loved anyone...
I finally had to stand up, because some guys wanted to park a truck
I stayed and watched them:
"let it out!
go on, go on, go on, go on...
a little more...more, more, more, more, more, more...
hold it! some more to the left...yo!
go on, yeah...keep on, keep on, just a little more...
o-o-o-O-K!
stop!
that's it!"

the sun was afloat in the arch of heaven.

                                            [A.J.S./I.C.]

Memory of an October Evening in 1984

I bring it to mind: it will be an October evening in the year 1984
in the Palace Square night will fall and the Great Bear, more and more
        tilted on its axis
will burn over the entire vault with a stone-silent flame, its flame
will reach the shop windows with watches and porcelain on the ground
        floor of the university library
and the glassy rind of the eyes which cross the street, which are
driving. its flame
will remind me of the coming of snow.

cold will come, bringing about on all of Europe's televisions
the same hallucinatory image from some film, possibly Canadian
plunging the population
into unfulfillment, into hysteria, into listening to the point of ecstasy
to the rumbling of the trams, to the scent of a cassette tape
to Bob Dylan's voice, Amanda Lear
glissandoing to snowfall, twilight, delirium.

I remember quite well what you will have on:
the cream-colored pullover which you will buy only next year and the
                checked pleated skirt
with heaps of jewelry glittering, sparkling, babbling, glimmering
jewels from the world's great museums, the pearls of the crown and soap
                bubbles patched in harlequin hues
and translucent crystal shoes.

it will be the end of October and your heels will click on the sidewalk
                under the Great Bear rotated over the Palace Square
your hair will be done up like a long time ago
you will think so intensely that the dense and reddish air will take the shape
                of diaphanous camisoles and icy miniature French perfume vials
I remember as if it were just a little while ago.

and since I remember your bluish, hedonistic, fleshy calves
reflected in limousine doors
I remember the continuous, chattering monotone of your hair
with uncut ends making straight to the self-service supermarket and winter.
I remember how we'll meet again by chance
in the landscape of a large city somewhere in the south-east of Europe.

and on hundreds of thousands of televisions concentrated in a few
        hundred square kilometers
a pair of dilated eyes will appear
and a pair of hands will prod the screen's gelatin
reaching for even a vestige of furniture to hang on to
plunging the world's population into misfortune, sterile speculations,
        paralogic in confusion
into cabals with the letters of your name combined on the lips of
        hundreds of millions
in hundreds of millions of frozen brains…

reaching for even a vestige of furniture to hang on to
cold will come, my skin brings it very sharply to mind.
it will be very cold in the square then and the scent of a snow storm will come
but it won't be snowing yet. you will pass by in autumn's twilight
absentminded as ever, and you won't even think of going into the Dacia
        Bookshop, or maybe at that hour it's closed.
and while exchanging a few words like some matte glass objects
I'll try to foresee how once we had been all right together
and how you had gone away under the flame of the Great Bear,
        time hurrying on,
while the library remained in its place in October, ragged
and fluttering.

                                            [A.J.S./I.C.]

Self-Portrait in the Flame of a Lighter

I'm a set of pulverized dentures, a mouth charred by a night's boozing
I'm a toxic pregnancy, a bifurcated torrent
of cyanide spurting blue from the spider's mouth,
stronger than a sperm whale, more fragile than a test tube:
I'm an incurable dreamer.

I'm a silhouette of braided firearms, harquebuses, flintlocks and mortars
I'm the apocalypse suddenly heralded
by all the sounding trumpets of the sewer pipes, the gas mains
when every flower becomes a Pearl Harbor of worms
and the worm poking its head from the grape
cries out, oh, God, your hawk would I be,
oh, God, cries the worm, were all the atoms of my flesh metamorphosed
        into light
I'd strobe the universe and your living creatures might at last gaze upon
        your countenance
and your hands with their infinite fingers, your breast with millions of nipples
the flame pouring down you like sweat.

I struggle in the gelatin of the ocean, in the dust of the earth's branches
in the mud of the sunset, in the lard of the dwelling places
I light up the lakes of an entire hemisphere
contracting a sunrise of golden ball-point pens out of my heart.
I'm the man spun of veins and bowels and electric wire
I'm a glass of bloody vodka
I'm an armor-clad bulwark of hotels burned to the ground.
I've rubbed my throat with algae, I've washed myself with a shoal of sevruga
I've had my teeth shattered in the sun, I've dwelled in women
I've dried my hair, after a bath of brambles,

with Grünewald's resurrection, with Caspar David Friedrich's sunrise
I've sucked a Molotov cocktail from a sponge.

crush me if you can, for I'm the one who
drinks your name and skeleton,
bone by bone, from the flask of flesh.
I devour your spider-webbed eardrum, as you loll on your hip
basking in bombardment, tanning from hell and catastrophe
I spin the cardinal points, I'm the puppeteer of your glands.
I'm the ulceration of a spring morning, and the tram stop spooled round
    by fog and blizzard
and the dinotherium skeleton which walks out of the Antipa Natural
    History Museum every night
lumbering about Victoria Square, clattering beneath the faintest stars
then along Stefan-the-Great Boulevard, flipping cars wheel-up to
    Cassiopeia and the moon
and scratching itself against the newly constructed apartment houses.
I'm all that ingests you and chews you to a cud and shreds you
an affectionate octopus, attached to your bulb and your brain.

…overwhelmed by loneliness, I was looking at the spectacle of the world
as if from a glass bowl.
amid flames, gasoline and tubes I meditated upon peace and purity
wallowing in a dough of alarm clocks.
shy, tinfoil, photophobic, I felt so good there in the cave
in the cave lined with blood.
then I saw the graves being dug up, halves of men and women
kicking to get out of the snowy earth
I saw blackened tank cars, lined with glass wool, drawn down a dead-end spur
under the most wonderful sunset of coiled angels
and a wild light howling to get out of the bark of trees

and gushing from under sparrows' wings.
God, what couplings then in campsites and artesian wells
what crowding in one-bedroom flats, and still such melancholy
on the faces of those walking hand in hand to the movie at the Scala.
I saw hell and heaven swirling skirts of crude oil above the cities
above the villages and the beehives,
rabidly fighting over a brick.
I was looking at all this with blue eyes, then I was forced to shut them
because, hair streaming, I passed through a defile of flesh.

I'm a cat thinking with a thrill of this universe
I'm a dreaming object, daffy with shop windows and traffic
I'm the mechanism in the tower, ready any time to set the blue and
          cherry-colored Marys
revolving above some girl or barrette
or above a city with bridges of hydrogen.
next to you I'm nobody, you, phantom charged with energy,
illusion more real than stone,
you who hold the world in your palms sheltering it from the wind
like the flame of a lighter, the golden world
that lasts only as long as you're lighting your cigarette, the curved,
          rotating world
full of plum trees in blossom, of circus tents,
of fertilizer factories and hairdressers and stockings
the world we love so much…

I'm a screw of dripping tears, a bouquet of vices and pulsations
a field across which my heart limps ahead on crutches.

                                                                         [A.J.S./R.S.]

Woman, Woman, Woman…

1

in the roar of this December morning
who flicks so much light from his fingers, so much light?
who causes these convulsive discharges, the flicker of bedside lamps, the
        automatic shutter-release of cameras in shop windows
in quest of chance, a specter, blood, tires?
who feels woozy with vertigo, seeing and touching with neither sight nor touch?
who attracts into the window of the Musica shop so many clouds of
        evaporated purple?
who splashes a huge glass of soda water on the exhaust-marble of the
        Telephone Building?
who enters frozen, transparent Bucharest wearing lipstick of flame?
who trails her dress across the electrical network causing the
        simultaneous lighting of branches in Cişmigiu Gardens,
            the transfiguration of the green fence railings, a tabor light?
who brushes with hip and purse the façade of the Universitas Club, the
        Amphitheater Review, purifying, exciting, polarizing the green
        halls where congresses of smoke are convened?
who brings sweet negligence to the lascivious eye of our contemplation
        which, in winter now, feels its lid more panoramic than da
        Vinci's last supper and heavier than Nazareth?
who casts the shadow of her little cutie-pie pout over auto bodies,
        covered with wounds, filled with terror and discontent,
        peeling off seven layers and crushing their engine?
who lets her tear fall on the velvet of my jacket, who was once livelier
        than the Lipscani Bazaar, more brilliant than the Boulevard
        Cinema, more tender than the Garden of the Icons Park,
        sulkier than the Yellow Sea when the weather clears and sharks
        can be seen circling in the water?

who scratches cassette tapes and assures the failure of weekend parties
	and name-day parties and causes them to end in boozing,
	gobbling fish sandwiches and just about no dancing while
	January witches revel on the balcony in their sabbath reeking
	of diamonds, moldering in jasper and coral?
who casts sharp shadows in the snow alongside the Press Building and
	the promenade by the highway?
who has plump cheeks shiny and dimpled but terrible as the cheeks of
	paranoia, death, decay?
who glitters, who dazzles, who moves one dainty shoe after another, her
	flowing hair changing color with hundreds of billions of seasons?
who floats, neck veins throbbing, immense as a statue of liberty and slow
	as in dream, over the midwinter night's dream of the city,
	with her many-branched nails prying into every drawer and
	removing pantyhose with runs, mildewed lingerie, moldy
	lipstick, scarlet-singed mirrors, dried orange peel, crumpled
	bank notes and elytra fallen from insectaria?
who exposed to our folly her naked vomer and bared her breast with its
	scorpion's barb?
who filled with lavender, sulfur, asparagus, flame, love, biscuits and
	carbide the trolley-bus I was waiting for at the Arsenal stop?
who suddenly starts to snow over the carpenters' workshops, over
	the grade schools, the kindergartens and finally over the
	synagogue perched on a Havana-Club sephirot?
who remembers my baby pictures with atropine-dilated eyes that tell us
	only: I know. I was aware. I learned?
who drives down the Boulevard of Victory in a limousine of guts,
	cartilage, ears and vertebrae, a fine smile drawn across her
	lips, but hiding a body as lustrous as a bomb, a tube of poison
	candy-drops?

who has the ring? who owns scorn? who is sold simultaneously in all stalls in
	the Union Square Market for a handful of sequins? who secretes
	a bioelectric field that can bend the crosses at the Resurrection
	Church, tie knots in the lights of the Republic Stadium? who
	with only a systolic murmur knocks down the acetone snail of
	Dalles Hall replacing it with a jet of water droplets heavy with
	rainbows and shiny candy wrappers and lemons?
who is my beauty?
who else can it be, my pretty one, my darling?
who are you, my love, darling, dearest?

2

under the firmament you're like a baby with a handkerchief shading its
	face, asleep in the tram
oh Lord, you tormented me, I tormented myself for you
I threw up, cried hysterically, dug my nails into my palm clenching my fist
	for you
wrapped myself in the curtain, tore it off, fell to the parquet for you
gnawed the pillow with my teeth only for you
chewed my obsession until my brain got periodontosis, letting its
	constructs wiggle loose and the idea of the infinite spiral
	upwards like a turbine of pink dough, like a rosette of little
	bones, like a morning star of toothache for you
and I dreamed that I was dragged from under my blanket with my head
	conic and bleeding and that I crawled to the middle of the
	room and my mother fractured my pelvis with her half-yard
	long shoe-sole only for you
ripped my cousin's pinky with my teeth when he was one and I was three, then
	laughed like a madman, like one possessed by the devil, for you
I went to college in your desk, lived in your city, witnessed my human
	condition fixing my eyes upon your belly, for you

I celebrated New Year's Eve hugging a huge cigarette lighter, rose into the air with it, flew out the window and soared over the city clinging to the cold nickel-plate until the stars knocked us onto the tram rails and a water-sprinkler truck dragged us to the sewer for you

I was witty for you, I wrote books for you, I bought myself corduroy slacks and a digital watch and chain for you

I was predestined for you, they vaccinated you against me and still I populated you like a spirochete, like a tapeworm, multiplying myself extravagantly for you, devouring your blood, your glycerin, your sap, your food, your fat, and I left you surreal and lean and nostalgic for you

I had intense ultramarine eyes for you

I died for you and I entered your belly and my teeth alone gleamed through the night of red. I split open an adder and then glass doors swung wide and above them in neon it said ELVIS I emerged under a sparkling blue sky full of dirigibles, beneath which there stretched a city with subways and monorails and shop windows full of musical instruments painted sweetly in mahogany, in orange, there were huge brass instruments, green drums, saxophones, transistor radios, turntables, and in the center of your canvas among dewdrops you were radiating like the Mystic Rose, so that citrus flames licked my face until I went away disfigured, cut to the bone, and your smile had bars, bars like in the zoo

I was lonely among steam locomotives, and suddenly I wished myself more human for you

I wished myself more masculine for you

all this year, the miserable year of 1980, my mind was one step away from abortion and I no longer believed in anything, especially life's capacity to produce pleasure and joy, and I developed canker sores biting myself for you

and I shredded my heart, diaphragm, lungs walking hour after hour along the driveway into the circus delirious and gesticulating to the lawn, the magnolia, the Pekinese, the lake with its filth, waiting for a connector cable to be plugged from between my eyes to the stellar cassette recorder

I sighed like Petrarch in the collar of my sheepskin coat coming back at six in the morning from some crummy party, where all the glasses had stickers with your face, and I wiped the whitewash from all the walls walking against garages, warehouses, railway stations for you

I had an operation for you, I got drunk for you

I alienated myself for you

I cultivated myself for you

I adolescentized myself for you

I bogomilized myself for you

I became the workshop where you ordered your gloves and the crosswalk on which you crossed to the Romarta Department Store and the Arab in his car who picked you up in front of the Continental Hotel

I was your grandmother's nervous breakdown the first time you stayed out all night

and I was happy even ultra-happy a whole rosy, sparkling evening, reading alternately Valentin Rasputin, Nichita Stănescu and *The Diary of Virginia Woolf*, and with the intensity of an epileptic aura thinking only of you

I was strong and cheerful and peevish and gossipy and tender and masochistic and conceited and green and blue and untamed and above all else handsome, handsome as the grin of agony,

    as the hubbub of the apartment complex, as the love dream of
     every nail in the hardware store
I meditated on the transmigration of souls and I lived under the earth of
    your tits blind as a mole lit up only for you
I was yours alone, all you had to do was yawn the Antipa Museum wide
    open to swallow me with a muzzle, trunk, snout, stinger, beak,
    jaws, molars, incisors and maxillae, rake me with your pincers
    and your chalicers and your tongue and your claw and the
    venom of your tail, electrocute me with your elastic cyanide skin
with your bouquet of chrysanthemums in your arms
with golden braids wrapped around the back of your head
and tied with a ribbon.

3

…there was so much light in the foundation on your cheekbones
so much fear in the hollows of your collarbones
so much modernity and nonchalance in your gait
so much *je m'en fichism*, such misfortune…
do you still remember me? who was mircea?
what years was he your friend?
do you still remember any of it? the way we used to walk past the
    armenian church
your hand in mine in the pocket of my overcoat
through the snow of murky streetlights
or when we climbed to the roof of my building among hundreds of
    antennas and linens
and way down below we could see only miniature houses and trams that
    glided along Stefan-the-Great Boulevard and high above were
    only the stars shining through the battlements of the Police
    Headquarters, and every now and then an airplane blinking red
    on and off in silence in isolation in fear, and oh, I want… I want…

who are you now? what's become of your nostalgia, your helplessness,
        your selfishness?
disburdened of you, my life rushed high above
and I can't breathe
I really can't understand anything
oh, woman, woman, woman
woman, woman, woman, woman…
now all I can do is wait for your phone calls,
listen to music, hang out with friends,
read some more, wander into a movie,
but I bury myself in an unbreathable hīnayāna
I don't want you back
rather, I wish you never left…
dearest, you were so sweet when you wanted to be witty, and when you
        needed love
who unbuttoned her own buffalo-plaid shirt?
who studied pedagogy with her glasses perched on the tip of her nose
        until she made herself feel sick?
who gave me the rhymes to write sonnets to her?
…now you belong to the physiological
now you're only a contortion in my fingers, a rupturing of tendons
now you're only a pool of blood where someone was slaughtered
on the divine snow in Bucharest,
now you're only a former fellow student
a sweet former fellow student from my college years, from my youth…

4

now you're a superstition, a hyperreality with tens of billions of faces.

        [A.J.S./B.Ş.]

Sonnet
["be careful when you step between tramcars..."]

be careful when you step between tramcars packed with little crosses,
    chains, cigarette lighters, creoles,
with the staccato ooze of radio plays, oh, my darling,
I hoped the mirror bracelet would fit you, Bob Dylan could've been high
    every moment of his tours
on your rosy neck scented with eau de cologne and tires
be careful about carelessness, tequila, pulque and other liquors, be careful
that your leg stays firm under the fabric, the spring
of the joint under the muslin
be careful with me, oh, my darling, don't let
the orchids and primroses of sweat effloresce through your zippers, don't
    abandon as yet
this wretched city with paving stones bandaged and tied with strips from
    your dress
be careful how you walk along the rails among stationers, confectioneries
    and haberdasheries
be careful not to crack your teeth on the antineuralgics' rubies or on pralines
be careful, the tram driver is wadding the buffers, is gnawing on pencils
is circling C. A. Rosetti's statue just for you and for Phryne and for all the
    lovely courtesans.

                                                    [A.J.S./R.S.]

Sonnet
["it seems you're made of cellophane, it seems you can be won at dice"]

it seems you're made of cellophane, it seems you can be won at dice
and lost through your woman's condition, then won again,
lost again, and won, then finally stuck like malachite in who knows
                what tie pin
it seems you weave fables when you cross one leg in front of the other
though the most delicate, you seem to deliver kerosene and solar cells
                with each indifferent, quick grin
though the coldest, the most informal, you drink the most
you prefer Cinzano with lemon, let's say, you dance as you wait for the bus
dazed with narcissism and grace
it seems you sip mango nectar in the sweet shop with a view of the sea
a view of the dolphins and of floating petits fours and cakes for tea
it seems you're a juggler under nickel-plated eyelashes with your sphere of
                hearty stupidity
it seems you know me, you've known me, your thong of smoky crystal
seems to have known me, your clogs of human *peau de soie*
when I ask each one about you, it simply says: *je ne sais quoi…*

                                                    [A.J.S./R.S.]

Sonnet
["then all at once you start to wonder"]

"then all at once you start to wonder
and it seems, no, it couldn't really have…"
it was a starry night
we had stopped in the middle of nowhere, the others got out
only the two of us remained in the brightly-lit car
I was looking at you in the rearview mirror
and from behind us a green being kept gesturing
she had come down from the stars
for it was a starry night
a being with no body
and no soul
"what is your name, green being?" I asked her
"my name's Viorica," she replied to us sadly, "little violet…
just call me that, Viorica"

[A.J.S./R.S.]

Bebop Baby

Bebop Baby ('Cause Tonight You'll Be Mine)

you were so highly evolved, such a flirt, a charmer and a skirt
that even the Adam's apple at your neck had descended
from the apes eons and eons before I found myself here
your little tit had emancipated itself to hyperboloid and sphere
ending in a sweetness and a toxin
of jailbait ingenuous and wanton.
gliding over vacant lots, you were a compound
of barbiturates, armpits, prisms and cellophane
levitating like a leviathan through the forests of Mondrian, under the trees
beneath which the atoms got scattered like china cups in smithereens
you're just like an armored mini-tank in the camouflage of syrup
and your figure reminds me so little of aesop
that I wrote you a bebop
and I'll sing you my bebop

hey, bebop baby, 'cause tonight you'll be mine
bebop baby, the stars, they're gonna reflect, refract and shine
not upon your sheets, not down your neck so fine, nor your pillows over
but on the dew dimpling your crumpled slip lying in the clover
yeah, bebop, oh baby,
dance, dance,
bebop!

you've revealed the universe to me: a handful of mint drops and spinning tops
a humdrum bit of dust, plants and gnawing animals, some
                thrumming whirligigs
with your little muzzle you've bitten my cerebellum in a kiss
and now I'm no longer able to breathe, to cough, to sneeze
to caress your conch shell, your hair bun
under your nails to dig toothpicks, Nat King Cole, Mahavishnu, Voronca
and Felix Aderca.
you said to me, oh, how you said it I'll never forget:
"let's sit a while on the bench and watch the sunset
you know, the Doppler effect has rather bizarre consequences
    just imagine, my love, that beyond a limit of twelve billion light years we can never hope to know anything more of this universe and that's because swarms of galaxies beyond that limit recede from us at a speed equal to or greater than the speed of light, and consequently the light signals, the photons, no longer can catch up with us. not only the light but also everything else that consists of electromagnetic radiation."
    we sat with our faces toward the arena of the State Circus whose big plate-glass windows reflected at various angles the multicolor breezes of spring getting tangled in the swollen buds on the spreading magnolias, moving the clouds here and there on the vast vault of the sky, fondling the pine needles tenderly and the delicate new green leaves of a kind of vine cork-screwing up the stalks of the neon tubes not yet aglow
    "surely, then, we won't know anything beyond that finite limit," I answered, looking at her beautiful head, her hair like an entanglement of burnished-bronze equations, her fine skin, protected by a thin layer of makeup base, her eyes big, yellow and glittering.

I couldn't concentrate, because, looking at her lips, I could automatically bring to mind their tasteless taste and almost savor their vague aroma, was it ether or maybe perfume from her lipstick? I would have liked to tell her that we did not know and could never hope to know more than the body of the woman we loved and her teeth touching our skin somewhere just below the clavicle.

I no longer was listening. but meanwhile evening had fallen and the pines had lost themselves in the isolation of a deep blue fog. the green needles had turned coffee-brown, everything was about to climax in a parade of stars. oh, and how you made your entrance at the tinkling of the wineglasses and demitasses
how you buzzed like a drosophila in a Bucharest of syrup
crooning you a doo-wop, from its every sidewalk a bebop
scatting with all its tapping footsteps this happy-go-lucky bebop

hey, bop, bebop
bebop baby, 'cause tonight you'll be mine
and your upturned face, it's gonna blaze and glow like wine
not with apathy, not with lackadaisical spoiled manners, nor misery
but big splashes of an oarsman in a galley
yeah, bebop, oh baby,
dance, dance,
bebop!

you were so rapacious, so voracious and ferocious
that even your sapphire earring had learned enough to be tenacious
and to smother, to snuff out, to suffocate

your adolescence sprinkled with chloroform and transubstantiated into a gag
chafes the cavity of my mouth
and the skin on my palms, together with my nails, fits tight like a glove
oh kill me, kill me
kill me
kill me
kill me
kill me

fill my flesh with amphetamine, turquoise, beryllium, faïence
turn me into tableware, make me into tweezers, a curler, a lamp, a vase
take my heart and dance!

hey, bop, bebop
bebop baby, sure, tonight you'll be mine
yeah, dance, dance,
bebop!

[A.J.S./I.I.]

A Motorcycle Parked Beneath the Stars

I'm a motorcycle parked beneath the stars, by the window of
        the television repair shop.
a breeze blows from the alley, I'm pale, helpless.
in the shop a bulb's been left burning, so that something like
        two cathode tubes
a few flowerpots with asparagus ferns and cactus, shelves in the corners
        crammed full of housings from TVs, AGFA cassettes and wires
glint obscurely, populate my solitude.
because I feel so lonely.
in my rearview mirror galaxies swim,
stars fog in globular swarms, transmit their panting to radio sources
all of them rushing farther and farther away in desperate flight, like
        criminals from the scene of the crime
leaving behind a trail of blood.

what silence. sometimes I wonder
what it means to make love. because that's all they talk about.
        every Saturday they mount me
and drive me along the highways. I can look at the hills, clouds, the sun
raindrops, the bedraggled trees getting tangled in rainbows…
oh my cylinders throb in such frenzy. then I feel I'm really alive.
they go into the motel and make love.
they are the Masters and feel free.
but how can anyone made of cells be free?
…and in the driveway out back by some dust-covered VW Beetle

I thirst for love. If I were at least able to love the plug on the extension
        cord in this shop window
I'd caress its white plastic skin with my fingers, if it let me
and if I had fingers. If I could at least be alive
in the bioelectric field of the cactus...
soon, soon I'm going to die, and I'll not have done anything in this world.
they'll toss me on the scrap heap
they'll smash my headlight, and its burnt-out bulb will dangle from two
        flimsy strands of wire.
all my life I've helped others to make love
and I'm going to die among induction coils, magnets and thistles.

I'm a motorcycle parked beneath the stars.
in the morning they'll mount me again, they'll twist my handlebars,
        they'll put me in gear
then once again on the colorful road, among russet hills,
        among blue mountains
in valleys threaded by meandering rivers
over railroad crossings, through crystalline country towns
racing against the wind through rain showers and exhaust fumes
eating the miles.
is this what they mean by making love?
anyway, this is my consolation, it's my calling, my love.
for this it's worth being alone.

[A.J.S./I.I.]

Gypsy Queen

I was listening to "Gypsy Queen" when she burst into my sight
an iron scythe in one hand, ten thousand fingers on the other
baiting the bulldog-headed clouds, the fanged thunderheads over
              the mountainous land
and when it started raining bubbles of lymph and bile and blood
she started barking, spewing lies,
guzzling my swoon from a glass as wide as the moon's span.

I was listening to "Gypsy Queen" when she burst into my instincts
crazy to high heaven, stammering out of her three billion breasts
her scythe slicing the planet Venus into a pair of transparent,
              dripping hemispheres
killing me with a turquoise lance.
her face between the sheets
was an asphalt floe, her fire-sewn belly jetted a fanfare of scars,
her foot, your own foot propped against the wall…

oh, Gypsy Queen, burgundy queen of Gypsies,
freest of the free, release me from behind the cell bars of your thorax
where I sprawl on your diaphragm guarded by your heart's bulldog
gnawing at each other, by turns gashing each other's throats in a bloody duel
in which my hundred thousand eyes, crematoria windows of sparks,
set the fir trees ablaze and leave the mountain bald.
I'm trying to escape, but I find monsters guarding every way
oh, jailer whose hair is fingers
I'd mine your every pore with a spike and a dynamite stick
to make you get the hell out of my loins.
To remove your fangs from the throat of my sleep.

                                          [A.J.S./C.H.-B.]

I'd Like to Be Your Friend

I'd like to be an electroscope
to spread apart your dainty legs
I'd like to be Maxwell's pendulum
I'd like to be Berzelius' beaker
I'd like to be Newton's law
I'd like to be your friend, my love, because there's nothing in the world
        better than love.

I'd like to be your friend
I'd like to be Basedow's disease
I'd like to be a Eustachian tube
I'd like to be the Champ de Mars
and Stefan-the-Great Boulevard's mother
I'd like, my love, to be your friend, my love, because, my love,
        there's nothing in the world better than love.

I'd like to become a cosmonaut or gangster
or a miner like my old man
to grow in your deep almond eyes
in your pearly teeth, your pomegranate lips
in your hip, your knee caps, your gemelli muscles
in your socks, your shoes
only to grow in the paving stones' eyes
only to have you call me sometimes…

I'd like to be Buridan's ass
I'd like to be Edison's bulb
I'd like to be Barbu's lackey,
Damocles' sword and your friend—
I'd like to be your friend, my love, because there's nothing in the world
        better than love.

[A.J.S./R.S.]

Little Elegy

love me, 'cause I love you too,
care for me, 'cause I care for you,
sun's yellow, sky's blue, clouds pale turquoise,
so, dear, let's enjoy this life

"…till the silver cord be loosed,
or the golden bowl be broken…"

the fields are green, the roads are deep in dust
the hills are golden, the brick viaducts breathe,
you're a sweet girl and vacation's almost over
your mother, she's an honest woman.

try to treat me gently, don't torture me,
don't give free rein to the aggressiveness in you;
keep ideas of marriage on a short leash, just let things flow,
and when you make love, don't believe you're making love.

I'm fed up with love affairs fraught with tantrums—
you must've had experiences like this too: biting the pillow,
> hour after hour of tennis to try to make yourself forget
phone calls when you're trembling as if plugged in—the hell with
those days, the hell with "my soul-mate," "my doll-baby"…

love me, 'cause I love you too,
care for me, 'cause I care for you,
so what if we're short of money, let's enjoy
this love, let's hurry up and live

"…till the silver cord be loosed,
or the golden bowl be broken…"

[A.J.S./M.S.]

The Beast

you're quite a beast! you've paused at the jewelry-store window.
someone like you simply shouldn't be allowed to roam free.
                oh lord, what a pair!
what nipples through the fox-red Coca-Cola shirt!
you're quite an animal behind the cell bars of your jeans, behind the padlock
of your bikini. the haunches of raw meat you need to swallow down,
purring like a lioness. you're, my God,
oh, you're quite a woman!

no wonder you're not for mortals.
so as not to die from your hair's strychnine
a man's gotta be armored in Citroën sheet metal, padded with banknotes.
now you're checking out your reflection in the window with women's watches
that flash sparks back to your face. so you'd prefer
a fashionable quartz watch? you're the type. seedily dressed men
and even two house painters in their spattered painters' whites,
caps low over their eyes, keep ogling you.

it's autumn on Moşilor Avenue. this tempts me to compare
your bottom to a harvest moon. to you, I'm a big nothing.
if I were awarded the Nobel prize, you'd be impressed only by the dough.
if I appeared on TV, it wouldn't make a difference,
or if I'd been born in Bahrain.

you're quite a beast! you've strolled on to the next store window:
Philips electronics at eleven thou, thirteen… you've pretty lips, cute makeup,
and if your eyes are clever or stupid, what does it matter?
you live your life shampooed, sprayed, a labyrinth of couture
and downy hands… you live aesthetically, you display gleaming teeth.
while I hunch over my typewriter
reaping only disgust.

a single tit of yours is worth my collected works
as you walk through the autumn along Moşilor Avenue,
thinking perhaps of the Dunhill in your pocketbook.

[A.J.S./R.S.]

Skeeter

Skeeter, even now, when we have nearly nothing to do with one another
I think of you from time to time, remembering
how petite you were, how prudent and shrewd…

now it's winter and I'm here all by myself

why don't you drop by my place? I still have vodka in the fridge
I've done all sorts of interesting things, I've seen films and exhibits
met former friends of ours, heard new jokes…
believe me, we'd have lots to talk about.
or we could trade tales about our pupils, bragging in turn about their stupidity
reading aloud compositions with ludicrous mistakes…
I've got some music too, we could listen to it…
I'm serious, you know you must believe me: I'd be in no mood to touch you

we could go out around five beneath the fluorescent clouds
your white sheepskin coat caressing the food-store window
through the plate glass we'd watch them arrange the pointy foil stars,
the cheap glass balls, the dinky rattling Santa…

we'll get as far as Romană Square
sliding on the glassy black ice,
mixing with the orange snowflakes under the city lights
we'll slip, we'll fall, we'll laugh at each other
we'll be on top of the world…

I mean it, come on, come to my place!

[A.J.S./M.S.]

I'm Smiling

a couple of dumpy housewives scowl at me.
then I realize I'm smiling,
smiling on the 109 bus on my way to work.
no doubt, I'm not making much of an impression:
a young guy with long hair who gazes out the window smiling.
but I was thinking of you and, as always, I smiled.
it's like a reflex.

I woke up this morning tangled in awful dreams of being flayed alive
knitting needles pierced through my teeth,
and this brought to mind grammar lessons.
the bus reeks of gasoline and undershirts,
and what can you see from the grimy window? apartment block after
        apartment block.

I was smiling, and I believe I kept that smile a good long time.
I remembered you in your stretched-out yellow T-shirt
and me in a T-shirt, too, a grungy one, as we brazenly entered the
        Bulandra theater.
the lobby was chockfull of stuck-up chicks
and guys in suits and ties.
we, we looked like we'd just hitchhiked from Woodstock.

at school the principal gave me what-for and the secretary
made threatening noises. the poor potted rubber plant had lost
        three-quarters of its leaves.
during class, as I drilled the kids,
I found myself smiling again. I had to
turn to face the blackboard.

                              [A.J.S./R.S.]

Adriana

about six I was at the newspaper kiosk.
it was a warm evening though September was nearly over
I was wearing only a light sweater.
I peered at myself in the bluish windshield of a Wartburg
I was looking my best and
feeling really great.
twice I asked the ice-cream vendor for the time
but the girl showed up soon enough.
I took her hand.
it was
really pleasant out, as I was saying, she wore overalls,
light-green overalls, and had no makeup on
short of some mauve at the corner of the eyes.
I wasn't in love with her.
but she gave me the illusion that I had a girl, that someone cared for me a
        little bit,
and anyhow I was holding her hand (a pretty-enough
chick, quite a looker).
we walked chattering together as far as the August 23rd Stadium, and
the parachutists' tower…but what I've got to tell you,
we sat down on the empty stadium's topmost curved row of seats
under the metal paws of the lights.
it was very pleasant.
she smelled faintly of sulfur, but she'd doused her hair with
Magie Noire. a young girl.
when it got dark, we found a spot under the electronic scoreboard
followed by the mosquitoes.

P.S. I forgot to say
that in fact she wasn't in love with me either
and never in her life had loved anyone
but we felt good with each other
and we had pleasant evenings together. really.

[A.J.S./M.S.]

Beer and Cold

the winter of '83, what a hard, persistent freeze…
bundled up, I'm walking on Barbu Văcărescu Street with the stars
        reflected in the ice
and from the traffic lights the glow congeals into a thick clear glaze
all the way to what used to be Adina Kenereș's house
where the buses stop for lines 88 and 90.
I'm headed to the Berlin to the red room upstairs for a beer,
harlequins on the wallpaper bats and vampires and ballerinas and cannibals
a porcelain bear, and a cigarette lighter on each of the small tables.
right there, beside the porcelain bear,
we'd arranged, I myself, Tudor Jebeleanu and Dan Goanța, to get together
so we wouldn't waste the Monday afternoon
a bit empty now since the Monday Literary Circle's dissolution.
the German waiter wearing a leather apron
and brandishing his guitar-shaped church key
pries open a bottle as big as the whole scene, and from it pours down
onto the carpet the evening's froth, silvery-brown.
we were smoking and drinking, gossiping about what if and what not,
        yesterday and today,
the books planned by the Letter Publishing House, posters,
        then *Paris Match*, Coșovei,
Lefter, of course Mr. Florin
Stanciu our buddy and Cristina, Dinu Serăru and Led Zeppelin
also Orwell, UFO's, "the third wave," when the next war would break out
who in fact did compose "Penny Lane" and the epic of the student
        Dospinoiu the idiot
the biggest blockhead in the class I'm the teacher of…
damn expensive coffee and evening unfurling its fabric high above.
Jebe came with an Olympus

Goanța brought a tome from Plato's opus
and was showing passages to me
I was building a Babylonian tower
of playing cards and a couple times an hour
would toss in some inanity.
then all of us calling out, the check, please! the check! the check!!!,
      our glasses empty
and in the heart of the crystal ashtrays rainbows sparked by reality
and us turning hundreds of pockets inside-out
producing a clinking of coins and many a crumpled-up 25-*lei* note
and to the W.C. and to the coat-check, then cloaked in fur caps and
      mufflers and outside to the street
in the yellow cold in front of Romarta
and walking home and see you later, old man,
so long, 'bye, guys, then kissy kisses…
…and beneath the evening stars of silk, the night driving tin taxis.

oh, you're gone, my dreams, you're gone! where do I start now to explain this thing? what do I say first? I was a dreamer, I never understood anything that was going on in the world. I lived as in a dream and now, here I am, forced to open my eyes. seven or eight years, a period in which I wrote three books of poetry, lived obsessed by poetry, was persuaded to fanaticism by poetry. I was terrified by only one thing, that one day I would in fact have to grow up, that one day the external would start to exist, that I couldn't get away with it much longer. I feared that the growing cartilage of my own imaginary would ossify and I would become a mature man, "one idea less every year." not even transformation into a rhinoceros would frighten me worse. the fact that at present many of my friends are married and have children seems to me not monstrous, but unintelligible, it cannot make room for itself in my mind, yet I know for certain now that I must be mature, the streets and ideas have started to materialize out of the fog and acquire firmer contours, desolatingly rectilinear. I can no longer think in several ways about anything. my metaphor machine has ankylosed more and more with every passing day. what can I do? I have to think differently, and I know that I can't lie to myself any further. I can no longer believe in poetry (at least the way I did until now). until now I've been happy when I found an image or a metaphor I liked and I really wrote out of inspiration, wholly dominated by my writing. now I feel the need to investigate the real world and tell the truth about it, rather than create little colored clouds. I definitely no longer believe in a poetry of stylistic effects, but I cannot find any other manner of making poetry. and this isn't all, socially I'm also someone else, entirely transformed from the me of a few years ago. to be able to say how many things I no longer believe in, I would need a list three times as long as john lennon's, and at least he could say, "I just believe in me." I go slightly bonkers when I consider that I'll have to get married and have children and join the Writers' Union and write a few more books and so on and so forth until the *exitus*. why should I exist? all these ridiculous things are paralyzing me and keeping me from my work. I also ask myself who I shall be in 1985, when this poem, maybe, will appear, and who will Tudor be, who will Dan be, who will anybody be in '85. I don't know, I don't know...

[A.J.S./B.Ș.]

Do You Know the Country Where Lemon Trees Bloom?

I'm waiting for the no. 26 tram at the stop by the State Circus.
the wide road looks golden and the trees are green, green and so full of leaves
that even a renaissance painter couldn't paint them all.
I'm staring at the girls in jeans and baggy T-shirts
JOGGING I read across one's budding tits—I twist around,
        completely wheel about
a no. 5 passes by and I run my fingertips over the warm, red steel plating,
        conceiving of a verse
and phrasing it: "this summer we've all become auto mechanics,
we're all repairing something under the clouds' body shop…"

it's the middle of May, it's summer and I'm becoming quite a wack
children bring their schoolteachers coarse branches of lilac
and cellophane-wrapped lily-of-the-valley
if you look at the sun you'll get jabbed in the eye
by slippery-mauve splinters, and on your retina
a glare of faces and violet ribbons with a bright patina.
you, oh glassy sun, you moon, oh hirsute body astronomic,
this summer we've all become a sort of auto mechanic,
we're all repairing something under the clouds' body shop
we're all unscrewing the flowers' axle shafts nonstop.

finally, after a series of 24's and 4's—a 26.
I push into the crowd and climb on, finding a place against the rear window.
the glitter of the street can make you feverish,
but your heart is cold, for you have no love
and in the shop windows you can't make out anything
and you can't write, only letters, dumb and useless.
I open Himmelmann's *The Utopian Past* bound in beautiful blue
and read about statues according to Goethean thought.

on my right, on my left, Bucharest is and is not.

[A.J.S./M.S.]

A Vodka at the Caraiman Bar

I once had this friend.
for him, poking a sparrow's eyes out with a ballpoint pen
and driving a nail into a sleeping cat
were one and the same, old hat.
once, from an apartment building roof, he threw part of a hospital bed
         frame, painted stark white,
onto the hood of a car.
he was brutal and vicious to girls. his overpowering obsession
was to tie every doorknob with cords in hundreds of intricate knots.
at night in his sleep he'd howl when he dreamed he found himself in a
         vast, deserted square
and felt lonely.
talking with him was like probing a moldy lemon
like putting your hand inside the sticky funnel of a spiderweb.
he was a repulsive child, thoroughly bad.
but when he grew up
you had to take pity on him, he became so awkward and helpless
got on like such an oaf with women
and he never looked anyone he was talking to in the eye.
by himself, alone like a dog. God knows
why such a man walks the earth.

I'm sitting upstairs at the Caraiman while I worry over the meaning of all this.
it's mobbed, the human species hasn't yet emerged from prehistory.
nor does it mean to. I'm drinking vodka, a bit spacy after so much time
        at the office.
every day I spend two hours on trams. I read less and less.
I pay and head down the goddamned stairs. I'm about to turn thirty.
thirty years old!
when I emerge from the glass door, a sleety squall slaps me against a
        shop window.
damn, before I make it home I'll be drenched to the skin.

                                        [A.J.S./R.S.]

I'm Given a Copy of "Howl" Signed by Ginsberg

at present he's America's best known poet, and those who were at Struga
(the big-name Romanian poets…) say "he's a popular guy"
as my mother would say about the movie stars whose posters she sees
        while waiting in line.
my parallels with him are rather extensive:
I was born the same year he published "Howl"
and that year he was exactly my age now,
namely, thirty. and next,
I read him in the "Beat Generation" anthology and began to translate from
        his work, and his special rhythm and hallucinatory imagery
        influenced some of my poems in a direct way ("Woman,
        Woman, Woman…" for instance, or, later, "Sun King," which is
        written on a song by Lennon, but no one noticed that).
I was obsessed most of all by the beginning of "Howl": "I saw the best
        minds of my generation…"
since my own generation had begun to make its move, if barely:
Traian and Florin, they'd read us poems with railroad tracks and tombstones,
Cușnarencu, he'd read us interminable poems, Nino Stratan,
he'd read poems set on the Moon,
Sandu Mușina, poems about a washing machine,
Romulus, some visionary stuff we then thought of as "prose,"
cigarette lighters and spray cans appeared in some of them,
        highways and gas stations,
and we devoted hour after hour to the advantages of the subjunctive
to types of beginnings, to endings with a "twist"
to the most effective layout on the page…

in all this there was something of him. "The Day of the Locomotive"
was a reminiscence of him.

I'm rereading "Sunflower Sutra": he and Jack beside him,
        both sad (the famous Ginsbergian "sad")
are sitting in the shade of a steam locomotive…
it's the same locomotive pictured on the back of our group anthology,
        Air with Diamonds.
I remember that day so well!
Tudor hadn't a gray hair in his beard
Traian wore winklepickers and a musketeer's little goatee
Florin had also decided on a beard as if he could be angelbearded
and Nino kept dissolving in wordplay…
we took photos of a Felliniesque wedding at the Basarab train station
we crossed the pedestrian bridge taking photos of each other
we posed on a broken rocking chair and in front of a leprosy-riddled wall
        and with a vending truck on which was written, right above us,
            "sausages, cold drinks, hotdogs" (I wonder how this picture
            will look years later archived in *Manuscriptum*)
then we arrived at the CFR switchyard, where, at the end of a siding
        choked with weeds
among broken embankment stones splotched with tar,
we found the saddest place on the face of the earth—
a locomotive with no wheels, collapsed on its belly
others still standing but somehow crippled, the plate-metal of the boiler
        eaten away down to the fiberglass lining
and above, a sky as if scrawled by a crayon…
we climbed up, smearing grease all over our jeans
we got into the cab and pulled the levers
we photographed ourselves in dozens of combinations (and another time,
we'd drive there in Wanda's green Trabant with the globe of gold glass
        that reflected the world punctured by my longish face and
            Florin would take more pictures of steam locomotives and old
            railroad tracks and blue oxygen tanks, stacked)

then home. ah, later, much later
I went there with Cri, in her little sundress.
we made out a lot in the cab.

last night Magda gave me a present
a razor-thin little volume: *Howl and Other Poems*, with an introduction by
        William Carlos Williams—
on the inside page, his signature, in black ink:
funny curlicues, like unraveled threads.
And below it: "8/24/86. Struga"
I was deeply touched, and later, looking at it again, I felt
how important it is to be a poet
how necessary it is to be a poet.
not rattling your tail, not a wannabe devotee of orphism,
but a human being, a man and a poet, an honest man
and a good poet, if you can be.
even more than the title poem, I liked
those "earlier poems," there's so much that's sweet and resigned and (how
        in heaven?) at the same time such exalted sadness in "An
        Asphodel" or in "Song" or in "Wild Orphan"…
as if the page of the sky had been scratched hard with the tip of a red
        pencil until the sheet ripped
as if a sparrow shot with a single bb had fallen in the dust and then gone
        on spinning like a top
as if the keys of your typewriter had suddenly vanished and instead there
        were knife points yet you'd still have to write your great poem
as if clouds inside reptiles had suddenly turned into vertebrates and after they
        rained what was left in the sky would be their decayed skeletons
as if the crazy, wise, rustling stars were donuts out of which, by means of
        eclosion, would emerge not butterflies, no, not butterflies

as if the doll of every little girl in the world, in every room in the world
        where a girl's asleep, would stand up in its corner, approach
        the little bed with automaton steps, bend low over the bed,
        and suddenly let out an unendurable scream
as if, one ordinary spring, all the flowers in bushes, trees and garden beds
        would bloom, and from the buds, instead of multicolored
        petals, would sprout black holes that slowly sucked in the
        entire street, a window with an old lady, a stroller
as if the galaxy were a clump of tinsel on the cosmic Christmas tree, full of
        electric stars and globes in excruciating colors
as if women were tarantulas
as if that portrait of Cristina photographed when she was a child holding
        a snowdrop bud had become the very emblem of sadness
as if never, never would a man have thought that he'd disappear, as
        if people hadn't invented the unified field theory and the
        artificial kidney and catastrophe theory and the Marechal Niel
        rose and the vacuum in electric bulbs

as if the entire universe, spaces inside spaces, eons inside eons, blood
        inside blood, rock inside rock, teeth inside alveoli, thinking
        clouds, heaven and hell, heart and brain, flame and ashes
were nothing but
                LOVE
desperate, unrequited
                LOVE
the only thing that
to man or woman, child or old man

never seems out of fashion
never seems outdated…

thin, squarish, modest little book
while here so many obsess over their collected works
a debut booklet sensibly printed
and inside—"Howl" (Help!
help! I need somebody—not just anybody—
I'm alone and I need you, *you*.
I want *you* to understand me…)

I'm thirty, Ginsberg's age and Hamlet's
for me it's a drama I'll never recover from.
I'd like to stop, I feel sick in this rollercoaster car,
I want out, I can no longer distinguish the world
other than as Borges' whirlwind.
I woke up from the dream in which
colors spoke
smells shed light
and the world was
a structure of glass and halvah
a vertebra of velvet
found by a vegetal Cuvier.

ah, the dream's over.
alas, it's all gone…

[A.J.S./C.H.-B.]

The Girl with Socks of Diamond

svelte as an icicle
she glides by on a bicycle
the girl with socks of diamond.
she has hair of diamond
a face of diamond
and a skirt of green brocade.
in this little girl's glass thigh
you can spy a mechanism with wheels that fly
round and a silver piston.
the wheels fly round
the piston dances
and the teenager advances
trailing her hair of diamond on Moșilor Avenue.

under her blouse of ivory
under the breast from which peek out
tiny round snouts of diamond,
she has braids
tied with metallic thread
and her ribs are of diamond.
but here, in her thoracic cage, she keeps a hummingbird.
on the bird's fourth floor is where I live.
I'm sitting by the window now, staring at oilcloth trees.

it's so nice inside her chest!
the sky is turquoise blue!
the clouds are made of colored Plasticine
such as, dear reader, it's possible you've never seen—
(perhaps you've never been loved by a girl…)
here the sun is of cartilage, the moon of porcelain
and even tractor drivers can quote Paul Celan by rote,
even dandelion and chamomile together
are painted Chinese style with a feather.

what a magic world! through the evening breezes
drive crystal and cinnamon taxis
and between the limousines squeezes
the girl with socks of diamond.
in her glass thigh
perhaps you can spy
toothed wheels and a silver piston
the wheels fly round, the piston dances
and the teenager advances
trailing her hair of diamond on Moșilor Avenue.

[A.J.S./C.H.-B.]

Letter with Armpits

you're a letter with armpits
when he delivers you, the postman always rings twice
I lay you on the bed,
slip you out of your envelope of striped polyester
unfold you and read you while I think
about the hieroglyphics of your eyelashes' India-ink.
I scrutinize deep precedents, profound verdicts,
until I arrive at a pair of round insignias
of red sealing wax.
it's evening in the room
yet I take the risk
of following my findings as far as the asterisk
and the entangled signature
of anthracite fiber
indecipherable
but very agreeable.
although almost completely obscured in darkness
I can still construe your ankle's P.S.
and after that, with my finger,
trace the Braille of your beige and coral mole
which tells a bizarre tale
about a unicorn and a virgin.

I can't make much sense of you, likely I don't at all understand.
your text gathers itself here into a little mound
and then somehow ends below
in a sort of fishtail.
you're a database
only curves and graces,
a mainframe server
only keyboard and fervor.
you seem encoded in an incomprehensible script.

what do I read? what do I bite? what do I kiss?
a love missive or a financial prospectus?
an incendiary manifesto?
a desperate appeal? a terrifying curse? a plea on bended knee?
a telegram that reveals a death unforeseen?
who are you? what's spelled out on your skin?

[A.J.S./I.I.]

Call Me, Call Me Today at Last!

I'm so sad. you won't be mine.
I knew you could never be mine.
 …and I'd constructed a dirigible of corduroy just for you
 …and I'd built a castle with pinnacles of Dylan records just for you
 …and I'd paved crystal highways with my fingerprints just for you
 …and I'd hunted peacocks with propellers of freesias just for you
 …and I'd begun to believe you could hold all the world cupped in the
   hollow of your palms and you could drink from it until you
   were satisfied and the whole night long constellations would
   burn in your throat
 …and I'd begun to hope for once I would soon be nibbling from the lips
   of existence
 …and I'd begun to hope I would rid myself of the plexiglas scythe
now everything lies in ruin.
I can't reach you on the phone and you haven't called me for five whole days!

I'd bought a monthly pass for all the lines on your palm.
I'd plied your coasts in cabotage for centuries.
I'd studied you putting makeup on your eyelashes and chromosomes in
   an oval mirror.
how you rouged the clouds, how you scrubbed the sun's cheeks, how you
   painted the towers' nails…

o my kitten, wise up:
you're no longer so little, come on down from your pale district of
                withered streets
don't go on lying, don't keep pretending, stop cheating on me.

I'm so sad. our love's not going to last.
you won't be mine.
…and I'd constructed a Bomarzo park with sulfur monsters for you
…and I'd designed my apartment building with padded shoulders in
                order to appear more imposing to you
…and I'd strung wreaths of snapdragons between medevac helicopters
…and I'd bought a frigidaire with the wings of tropical butterflies
…and I'd begun to believe I could drain time and then walk in my rubber
                boots on the puddled and empty streambed where time had
                flowed and I could gather all the fantastic fish that had been
                swimming in the water of time, the fish with skeletons of watch
                hands, with ears of photographs, with a heart of human eyes
and I'd begun to hope I would crack death's shell between my teeth
and I'd begun to hope I would see your footsteps, I'd hear your skin.
everything's turned to dust.

oh, call me today, call me today at last!

                                                   [A.J.S./I.I.]

My Life's Getting Crowded

how many images I made when my life was empty!
it was a sensory deprivation, an obsession like that of Zweig's chess player.
while I was writing the *Love Poems*
there was nobody, absolutely nobody in my life.
I would stroll like a mad man on Magheru Boulevard whistling Lennon's
"I'm just a jealous guy," but I was jealous of no one
for there was no one: Jebe didn't make phone calls,
with Traian I'd had a falling out.
I wanted so much to have a woman of my own, a house of my own
(in the evening I went to the Volga Cinema and shed tears over every
        dumb thing).
I once told Emil at The Romanian Book: "You know,
I really suffer from loneliness." He looked astounded,
and I wondered what it might be like not to suffer from loneliness; since tenth
grade that hadn't happened to me.

for about a year my life has been getting crowded. everything is realistic
and flat like a photograph. I have a woman.
I have a house. I have (if not friends) buddies.
every night I read. I rush to work on the 21 tram.
but I'm not happy and I'm jealous of the lonely.

oh my loneliness—I meet you sometimes
as in the street (near a dairy bar) you might run into a former sweetheart
who once meant everything to you
and from whom life kept you apart.
what's left to say to you? you remain just as beautiful
but now you're a stranger to me and I can't have you anymore
and I can no longer press my face to yours except through glass,
        like Delon and Monica Vitti in *L'Eclisse*
now you're somebody else's loneliness
and I'm a man lonely for loneliness.

                                      [A.J.S./R.S.]

Eye to Eye

We're eye to eye, but I don't know: like two lovers
or like two spiders? like a man in a mirror? or like two blind faces
in an asylum? we're heading the same way.
You regulate my oxytocin, my vasopressin. I search
like a telescope mirror to capture you
on a few millimeters of life. It's as if
a trichophora larva were essaying to understand not man
but the worm. Shall I say that you're a god? That you're all there is?
        That's talking nonsense.
Your most minute pore is everything and more. And nonetheless
the eye of the gas burner or this instant when I'm clattering the
        typewriter keys
is greater than you, because they *exist*.

I imagine myself with the perspective of a bacterium inside my own body:
there, in my intestines, the digestive papillae
seem inconceivable quasars. If one of them possessed understanding
it would believe it understood *me*.
I fancy myself vaster than the universe and studying a photon:
I'd suppose I knew you.

So naive they are, then, the religions, mandalas, koans,
the paths to enlightenment and the Taboric light,
the magnum opus, the curious "life one day at a time"
of Zen Buddhists. What remains out of all these—beautiful literature.
Swedenborg, Novalis…mescaline, stylistics, ether,
the perfume of the lily, hormonal stimulants
are simply tricks: everything is psychic, nothing *real*.

Techniques of breathing
one hand clapping
letting go into the flow of life, re-experiencing oneness with the world
extinction, all allegories, deliriums, dreams
are just a hopscotch of the mind, computer games, phantomatics.
Many are the astrologers of the brain.

9:20. I'm writing in the kitchen. It's a cloudy May morning.
All seems so real, natural: an alarm clock, a sink.
But the flowering lily-of-the-valley stalk doesn't believe in my existence.
Nor do you, you who are reading me after so many years.
If you saw me in a video I wouldn't seem unreal to you any longer.
All the same I exist, I have a pulse, I harbor my own imaginary.

You're on both sides of my life, like a line on a Möbius strip
you're my parents and their child, like in Klein's bottle
you're like a parasitic crab, with its veins thrust into my veins
its face thrust into my face, identical to me and integrated into me,
you're in each object, because each object is a part of me,
uomo universale.
We're eye to eye, because your eyeballs
are in my eyeballs, and my image of the world
is identical to your image.

But in exactly the way
a written page looks identical
to both the learned and the illiterate.

[A.J.S./R.S.]

You Always Astound Me

    you crush me stamping my skin with your seal of approval
    you deafen me with the shock wave of your laughter
    you humiliate me by being
    you astound me by never existing
    you bestow death upon me, magus kneeling at my manger!

    you overwhelm me safeguarding me from beasts and mankind
    you flay me caressing me with an astral erysipelas
    loving murderer, leave me, leave your woman!

    how your heart throbs for me, your heart which is the universe!
    how it shrinks to an electron and the even more infinitesimal
    then explodes again in a wild orgy of light,
    your jealousy's yellow rose!

    death is my most cherished dream, my holy grail.
    now a million diseases adorn me
    with a bride's gossamer veil.

                                                         [A.J.S./I.I.]

A Crown of Thorns

I need you so much…eyebrow pencil of contemplation.
I long for you, I yearn for you…carotid of the shade.
I'm terrified…scythe, crazed scythe that chops off fingers,
lops off snail horns, sons.
love me, little sister with warm cheeks,
caress me, o caress me.

tears seep out from under my nails.
I too wear a crown of thorns
and have thistles in my beard.
a thin sliver of salami on a slice of bread.
a woman.
a life.
I won't become incarnated into even a spider, I'll be only dust, chalk…
I won't ever look around again.
I'll no longer know that I'm living on a bullet
which is insinuating its way under your nipple.
that wound, your wound is my life's tunnel.
your sudoriferous glands are suns, your fat, the moon,
your capillaries are stars, and soon

I'll erupt from your back, with splinters of shoulder blade,
soiled with marrow...crazy,
crazy in my lucidity.
mother, your death is the price of my life!
your dry breast is my rationality!
from the crown of thorns you put on my head
when I was squealing dirty with meconium
when I'd barely passed beyond the boundary of your mouth
the spines keep growing longer.
galaxies thrust into them like beetles
white dwarfs like ladybugs.
my head is encircled by the cosmos
pulsars flash on my nose, my eye sockets, my cheekbones...

oh, take me in your arms, hide my face in your folds
astral sister, you who never,
nevermore...

[A.J.S./R.S.]

Mircea Cărtărescu in the Fall of '87

I.
mircea cărtărescu.
a prisoner of myself. I, a "regular guy"
mixed with gastric juices and MAO inhibitors. I,
a dreamer, a consciousness.

I was formed in an intact uterus, in a milk bottle.
I opened my eyes (rheumy), and I laughed
with bare gums at 40 days old.
I remember mother: as imposing as the party press headquarters:
        ragged clothes
and the penny of her coffee-rose nipples
like a badly scarred burn.
I, m.c.,
learned to interpret the color splotches
to cut through the roaring with a blade (and
to use my larynx). I
dreamed city districts under yellow skies and statues of brass
and I grew as many fingers as there are stars in the galaxy (rubbing them
like a fly, I stretched my wings)

broken teeth, lost fillings,
asymmetrical eyes, a spider's history
and now? look—it's fall here along the Colentina Highway
and the trams painted in their stained yellow clatter between apartment houses
and everyone is buying bread. I feel sad.
sad. I'm wearing out my threadbare jeans against the steps of an
        apartment house.
(a guy with a stroller enters a pastry shop). yes, I,

a fellow someone made fun of: can you see it, kid, over there?
what's the spiral shining up there? that's the caramel. what tosses and
        howls upon which
pass cargo ships? that's the sea. and high above, those are the stars.
there existed Aristotle and Edison. 2,000,000 species are known
there exist sixty ways to make love and fifty ways
to leave your lover.
adolescents got "feelings."
anthrax is atrocious.
mirrors and paternity are abominable.
there exist two social systems and a third world,
also there exist in your memory Felicia's (your schoolmate's) mouth
and the screwdriver you repaired the iron with two days ago.
there are green fields and Goethean thought and differential
calculus.
bees are
computers are
being
is
take a look, young puppy, the world…The world!
THE WORLD!!
can you see? there's light
and there exist books and women. some you'll fall in love with and
(because nothing should be neglected) you'll penetrate them, with the
        brain or with
the sex. but

no. not a word about
destruction, getting crushed. I'm a man
and can crumple up the universe and stuff it into my mouth as the littlest
        baby stuffs in

the head of the rubber snail. and the roof of the mouth gets filled with stars
where as in *Pantagruel* live people
who contemplate my canines with large radio telescopes. I.
mircea cărtărescu. 31 years old. a teacher. married. one child (a girl).
I've been cheated since I was an axolotl,
a latimeria…
just as you squeeze a sparrow nestling between pieces of
           cardboard packaging
so you clutched me in your stevedore's paw
and I was cheeping and you raised
my sweaty wing (with tiny
sheep lice beneath it)
and switched on the sun and in eight minutes
I started to believe I exist. you. you!
a man who doesn't own anyone!
a woman not owned by anyone!
ah, look, old man: colors, a frenzy of forms, reverberations
gushing fountains, abstruse palaces (at the Buftea Studios) savages
(in Mato Grosso) quasars
(far away, in the metagalaxy), all kinds of things: what with thought
you can't reach, glass! balsa! concrete walls? ! rainbows!
heroism! freedom! but the star

the black star of death
there where all the lines lead (in the palm), there
where all fossils go, where every Ramapithecus
is heaped, where
all the people who have ever lived
are scattered like seeds, the big star
which nourishes itself on tongues and gullets
the black star of happiness

                              upon it
never...
            never...

I sleep with my own imaginary
I bite its paps, fecundate its uterus
and the fall passes by (the earth, leprous,
creeps across the pastures of paradise, the earth
full of the rot of man and root plants), the winter too and
the spring, and
the belly of my imaginary
swells like an eggplant on the petiole and then cracks
and there emerges...emerges...

you

who hold the star
my black star
between your palms and crossed knees. oh, no, I don't believe
any religion can explain it!
any myth!
it's only you
aubergine-violet, puling, but with the Gypsy-Sibyl Mafalda's eye
with a diamond on your forehead, with placental liquid
streaming along the spine.
as big as life
with flayed skin
with organs in plain sight.

you, before whom I am
dead.

I.
mircea cărtărescu. who can sleep
and knows how to digest. and exists.
(today, Sept. 12, 1987, I'm alive)

[A.J.S./R.S.]

Prisoner of Myself

How It Is

Once I used to rack my brains to bring forth an essential line.
Every day I stared down death and despair.
I thought, really thought hard, about "the immortality of the soul."
Long ago I used to be inspired, I'd have visions
I wouldn't have traded places with Nichita Stănescu or Dylan Thomas
I wanted to be an *uomo universale*.
Until I was twenty-nine
I wrote real poetry.
I let myself grow thin, I turned gaunt so it would flourish.

Now I take Chinese vitamins and lift weights.
I don't want to go mad.
I don't want to be a monster in inspiration's clutches.
I don't want my poetry to outlive me.
Now I listen to music and push my daughter's carriage.
Now I know: this is reality.

I couldn't care less if you claim I've fallen to ruin
and outlived my own poetry. That's what I want.
The hell with my poems. I'm more important than poetry.

Do you know when I understood I'd become different, that I'm no longer
        what I was at twenty-eight or twenty-nine?
It happened one afternoon while I was working on some statistics for the
        Youth Defense Training Corps
and my mind kept flying off to crazy notions, to immortality.
Exactly then it got into my head that I didn't want to be immortal
all by myself,
that I'd no use for immortality
if Cri, if Ioana, couldn't live forever, too…
This was something totally new for me.

That's more or less what I have to say. As for the rest,
        any irony
        is up to you.

                                    [A.J.S./R.S.]

Clouds Over the Building Across the Street

I just can't move the compass needle by concentrating.
I've tried. I don't have the power.
I can't transmit the image of a playing card. I've tried.
I wanted to levitate and lay on my back drenched with sweat
          on the unmade bed
concentrating my thoughts for half an hour and more until I felt I'd go mad.
In the metro I tried to make this girl look at me
and it goes without saying she didn't.
God, I'm not one of your chosen.

My mind can't change the world.
I don't have enough love, enough faith.
I don't have a saint's aura around my head.
You deigned not to manifest yourself to me or grant me a sign.

I lay my fingers on the oilcloth table cover:
it simply won't yield, transform to reddish smoke.
I touch my little daughter's curls:
they are soft, golden-brown.
Nothing is different from what my senses tell me. Illusion doesn't exist.
My mind is a plane mirror to the world.

A plane, flat.
No scratch.
No previous life, no ectoplasmic being.
Neither Agarthi nor Shambala,
no Maya, to say nothing of dreams:
mere cosmetics applied to nothing.

As if hypnotized I stare into the flame of the stove.
I know I once lay inside a uterus.
I know I'll lie inside a coffin one day. Or I'll smear the earth with my blood.
I won't be the one to find the fissure.
In that group photograph *I* won't be the one to turn my head.

[A.J.S./D.M.]

I Beg You

eventually you're going to kill me
the purest of thinkers you're going to kill like a dog
and the holy man you're going to kill, yes, him too,
as if he were a flea-bitten stray crouched at the apartment-house entrance.
so many times I've told myself, "I wish
I could die this very instant
I'd consent to being killed
if it would happen suddenly, right away,
without pain…"

I once saw a beer-bottle cap
on the asphalt—I was returning home at two in the morning—
and I convinced myself it was the button that would blow up
everything—the world, the night, absolutely everything:
I closed my eyes and pressed it hard under my foot.

I've lived life
I've understood as much as anyone
you can kill me now, it's all the same to me, whatever.

but don't crush me between the elevator and the floor
don't let me fall from fifty feet
don't smash my pelvis on railroad tracks
don't leave me bound, naked, my head in a black hood
on the torture chair
don't burn my hair and skin in a chemical warehouse.

do it without intestinal blockage, without peritonitis
without cancer of the larynx, without AIDS
without my eyes plucked out of their sockets
without living teeth pierced by a dentist's drill
without blood gushing from my nose and ears.

don't make sport of me, don't nail me to the cross, don't castrate me
don't pull out my nails, don't run caterpillar tracks over me
don't break my neck, don't fracture my vertebrae, God,
if you will, if this is in your power…

I'm afraid of suffering,
I'm terrified of all atrocity
that's my weak spot—I'm a poor frail man
a poor scared rabbit.

what's in store for me the rest of my days?
am I going to know jealousy, depression, an inability to write ever again?
a painful old age, loneliness?
remorse for having taken the wrong road?
I'm afraid to scribble down the other things, lest they come true.

let me die quickly, painlessly.
and do it *now*, if you will, this very instant
let me feel nothing, I beg you, that's all I ask,
let me not have time to feel a thing…

[A.J.S./D.M.]

Sábato Would Have Taken It for an Omen

a cold bright April morning
we're in the Year of our Lord 1989
the trolley-bus 66 barely crawls through the traffic
in my seat, I'm reading *The Black Spider*
now and again I glance out the window at the colorful crowd
and feel irritation growing in me;
it's going to take half an hour to get to Kogălniceanu Square
I'm on my way to see the cover of my book of prose
and I've imagined every sort of possibility.

C. A. Rosetti's statue also has its own seat
and it's reading something too
part of the traffic of this entire earth unto "eternity"...

and then I noticed the creature—a girl
like any other girl, you could say
neither very beautiful nor very ugly
a tartan dress, patterned knee socks—a familiar style—
walking slowly in the opposite direction to the 66 I was on
she was some seven months pregnant
maybe that's why her face looked rather pale but with only a few faint blotches

the melodrama comes later, but can the real,
that which I saw with my own eyes, be melodramatic?
life is one thing, literature another
nevertheless, here goes:
this girl had no arms, only two stunted little hands
like a child's attached to her shoulders
like two little small wings of reddish flesh.

no doubt in my adolescence this would have made me look away
but now, in my corrupt maturity
I began to think anew about Stanciu's cover
about my book's coming out
while tying to see whose exhibit was hung in the lobby of the
       Very Small Theater.

                                              [A.J.S./D.M.]

Women

"women are fascinating
under twenty and over thirty—yeah
five years or so earlier, five or so later
what kid, when he doesn't yet know what the objective looks like,
wouldn't want a woman in her thirties?
what balding guy at thirty-five to forty wouldn't care for a young thing?
when you have a fat one, you want a thin one—because women are fascinating
a little below the waist and a little above—
when you've had a lusty wench, it's as if you immediately want,
        I don't know why,
a bashful maiden who'd ask you to turn out the light…"

Mareş and Dinu (may he rest in peace)
over a drink in the kitchen at Dinu's one night
at one of our generation's parties: "Look here,
the finest thing in the world is to put it to a woman, so forth and so on,
        this way and that"—for two hours they kept on talking like
        this, with all the details, the tomcats…

"women are actually just like us
they're as curious as we are
you know, you watch one on the street or on a tram
and wonder: man, what would it be like… ?
that's how they think, too.
and the same as you find men as shy as little girls
you'll find girls quick at the zipper
when they're alone with a guy."

Radu (at Rahova one cold night
over a mug of beer, even colder):
"Twenty-four? Seriously? By the time I was twenty-four
I'd had my fill of broads, I'd had legions…"
and then, playing with his lighter: "Look here,
you can be what you like, but a real woman won't stick with you
unless she feels you can tame her
you can be the biggest big shot, you can be a genius,
but fuck 'em and to hell with 'em…"

"women aren't human beings
you can't understand them
you'll find that out after marriage
you'll see how the little dove will take wing
how she'll yell at you
how she'll boss you around…
it's true that then
it won't be the same thing.
after five years of wedded life, when you lay your hand
on her bottom, it's like putting your hand on your own."

Mr. Nichi, in Berlin (Traian and me
listening to him over shots of vodka):
"It's the same with women: when you see one in the street,
the seam of her stocking a little cockeyed,
you'll know there must be something loose about her,
she's approachable.
Perfect correctness is inhibiting, both in a woman
and in a work of art."
And we: "Excellent!
Excellent, Mr. Professor!"

"both gorgeous women and ugly women
are OK.
beware, however,
the ordinary girl in blue jeans and a T-shirt
neither ugly nor beautiful,
who stands patiently at the tram stop.
she's like you and she's waiting for you."

[A.J.S./D.M.]

Oh, Natalie…

When I was a lot younger I had a crush on Natalie Wood
(even today I still believe that of all actresses
she's the most worthy of my love).
I give myself high marks
for not having become infatuated with B.B. or worse, God forbid,
        with Marilyn—
such shame has never stained me.

But Natalie Wood is really rather respectable.
I was in love with Natalie Wood.
We'd go for a stroll together in the evening in the
        Arsenal-Infantrymen-Dionisie Lupu neighborhood
I'd drape my arm around her shoulders and she'd hold me by the waist
it was a very beautiful autumn.
She didn't mind that I was in my high school uniform.
"Mircea," she'd coo to me, "Mircea,
you're so wonderful,
everything an intellectual woman could ever want."
"And you too, my little kitten, you're wonderful."
We'd walk on through withered leaves, no one understood us,
we were too sensitive, too different…
"Natalie," I'd say to her,
"oh, Natalie, Natalie, Natalie
your name's so beautiful… you know, Natalie,
today I'm nothing,
while you're famous, you've got a whole filmography behind you,
but I'm going to work hard, Natalie, you'll see,
I'm going to make the big bucks…"

And the autumn evenings were so sad,
the eyes of my sweetheart so deep…
It began to snow a little
and the trams flashed green at the contact with wet wires.

Then I'd already achieved glory, made money and women
I'd been published in Paris and Chicago
Out of habit, I'd still go back to Cantemir for sentimental reasons.
Every evening Natalie would be waiting
at the high school gates in her little Porsche
and we'd go for a spin down the Street of the Prophet,
        Corporal Troncea Street,
back on the Street of the Future.
I recall that one night
she parked the car along a sidewalk
lit a cigarette in the dark, and, with her sensual voice
(but hoarse and bitter then)
she confessed she'd cheated with a man. "Mircea, I *had to*,
had to tell you,
I couldn't have continued on, otherwise. You know,
not for a single moment did I want to go to bed with Robert
but he's so insistent… these blond guys are just awful…
but believe me, Mircea, believe me, you're still the best…"
I forgave her.
What you can't forgive a fallen woman
you must forgive a superior one.
"Cheat on me with your deeds, but not with your thoughts," that's all I said.

Then I had to leave for the army.
Daniela came to Cristi Teodorescu almost every week.
The very girl he's now married to would come see Mera.
Somebody even visited Romulus once.
Natalie never showed up for me.
On Sundays I stood like a dumb jerk at the guardhouse
and ogled the others kissing their sweethearts
and squeezing hands across the table...
When we cleaned the weapons I furtively read *Cinema* magazine,
I clipped out everything about her. About Her.

For ten years I hadn't heard a thing of her. Life kept us apart.
Then, maybe a week or so ago, as I was looking for blank tapes,
whom should I see at The Crystal Disk, near Lipscani Street?
Natalie! Natalie was back in Romania!
But she'd aged so much... I didn't want to talk to her
so I left before she might notice me (outside waiting for her
was that straw-haired Redford with his Cadillac).
Broth tastes dull heated a second time.
No, Natalie,
you made your choice, go your own way.

And yet, when I got back to my villa,
why did the seventeen rooms seem so empty?
For a long time I stared through the frost-covered window at my pool
in which a dead leaf floated...

[A.J.S./D.M.]

The Scent of Dry Leaves

the scent of dry leaves…
I once had a girly-girlfriend…
I was in high school, and one time I told her
just to act crazy (I was a poet), "you know,
I can see a whole lot more colors than everyone else." then she,
M., replied, "what? why don't you
go to an eye doctor?" but for real,
no joke… the scent
of dry leaves burning in piles in the courtyards, on Barbu Văcărescu Street
somewhere near the Energetics Institute…

those days I used to bedeck the fall with diamonds: this babe
appeared to me with hair (or gloves?) of diamond
all was diamond at the time
if people were shitting
they'd squeeze out diamonds, clinking into the crapper, and
if the trees had leaves, they had to be
of diamond.

I'd weep typing poems
but the women in them were all fancy-fanciful
I didn't know how to make love, I'd tried
as a kid but didn't succeed,
a jealous, bird-brained kid… a member of the Monday Poetry Circle,
a student…

it's sweet to caress a girl between her legs
when she's naked and very, very human
not "a woman"
and when it's fall, if the window were diaphanous

the scent would drift in from outside: dead lea-leaves
and red tongues of fire
in the courtyards…
sex is nonsense in books and movies—the heat of
fucking'n'sucking—
that's crazy
when actually it feels sweet and sad
bodies so serious
there's also fucking'n'sucking
but usually
most of the time
it's… different, it's…

Mir-Mir, that's what she purrs to me
but when I'm moody, she'll meow
to me Myeor-Myeor.
in the elevator, when we return from out in the city
and the light bulb has been swiped again
I grab her ass and growl fiercely, "got ya',
you're not gonna escape me… I'll rape you!" and she joins the game:
"get your hands off me, mister, or I'll punch your lights out"
and next our door
we unlock it
here we are, home sweet home
and we can turn our backs on everyone and everything…

and now, ladies and gentlemen, the great master of the endgame
of a poem, will give you his
perfect ending for a poem:
"oh the scent of burning leaves,
book-leaves burning in the courtyards,
diamond leaves of my book *Air with Diamonds*…"

[A.J.S./D.M.]

A Very Good Poem, with Satanic Sadness and a Montgolfier of Despair

now begins the despair of summer days
when, head in hands, you sit on the cement stairs
at the entrance to the building
and the workers' kids stare at you
as at a monster, who knows what movie you're in…
now begins the madness of yellow urine
that streams down from the heavens
now begins the heat that makes it impossible to breathe
inside autos.
I can no longer live this way
without believing in anything, without being anything,
with only the torpor of summer days,
the torpor of summer days.

I feel pity for myself
I no longer know anything, no longer understand anything
I feel pity for my spine
for the tiny hairs and pimples on my back
I feel pity for my poor brain
a Montgolfier of despair
withered like an elder flower
like an elder flower…

now begins the satanic sadness of rug beating
the bellyaching of the retiree as he repairs his little Dacia 1100
the madness of the Gypsy who climbs out the window,
        one boob hanging down,
glares at the clouds and shouts something.
summer begins,
the most grotesque cosmic object
a summer of Plasticine and sweat-dirt.
will I ever be something?
thirty-six years old, long hair, blue jeans
does God still watch over me? does someone still
love me? would someone really care
two cents about me?

a "Montgolfier of despair"—what bombastic shit!
"satanic sadness"—stupid, stupid!
oh, reader, receive this moronic poem,
you who often are shocked at good poems.
I pity you,
poetry-loving goose,
adolescent half-pederast.
come on, strut your ass and window-shop,
go take a walk in the Baneasa Woods,
put down this damn book!

                                                        [A.J.S./D.M.]

Once I Had Visions, Now I Have...

beauty will assume whatever form it takes
or it won't. so be it, I guess it won't.
in the morning
(after the night had smelled of snow and, on Colentina Highway,
the taxis' headlights and my very breath had frozen as I walked home
in my leather jacket)
Cri called me from the dining room, where she'd been fooling around
with the tape player—
"Mir ! it's snowing!"—
and I rushed to the window: for real, it was snowing
tiny flakes falling, and suddenly from the room
John's voice boomed out: "I'm a loser!
I'm a loser!
and I'm not what I appear to be"
the climbing vines coiled around the speakers
the books on the shelves
and Kitty's face, gorging herself on cookies (Kitty
without makeup is still Kitty) and above all
the cold in the house...

what was I saying? that it was snowing,
tiny flakes falling, on the tape Lennon was singing...
and I didn't care about anything or anybody, I was listening to music
and thinking only that it was snowing, tiny flakes sifting down

something welled up within me, and I wished
oh God, I wished that once I might
rid myself of that happiness driving me insane
so I could be my old self again!

…but I'll never be my old self again
because… John had finished singing
"I'm a Loser" and was saying now something like
he'd caught his girl with another guy,
a big deal, "no reply."
Cri got into the bath and I stayed to keep an eye on
the bucket of water heating on the stove
and behind the smoky glass of our cupboard the photo of the two of us on
          the locomotive
went smoky too, thawed…
I stuck my head out of window. Oddly wet snowflakes touched me.
I recalled my adolescence
when I walked to the trolley-bus stop
on Batiștei Street, when I felt I would suffocate with loneliness
and when, in winter, I came home at dusk holding her little hand,
and when I would type poetry…
when poetry meant something to me…

and yet… God,
when it snows,
when you go out in the frozen streets…

                                                    [A.J.S./D.M.]

I'm Jealous, Damn It...

I'm jealous. It's no use, I know it's not pretty,
yet I'm jealous and it's petty.
I'm jealous taking a shower,
grinding coffee, returning from work at any hour
in the rain
while on an LP Baniciu sings a refrain.

I'm jealous combing my hair, pulling up my jeans
appearing on TV, or watching the pedestrians
who glance at the Central University Library.
Or in front of the Hotel Bucharest when I see the girls who never are shy
and take cash from the boys
to be their toys.

I'm sorry, love, this is how I am, I can't be any other way,
I can't get over imagining you in someone else's arms
can't get a grip on my inner monster
can't keep from griping when you're late…
I worry when you're too happy
I seethe when I see you're sad
and I think: Damn! she's gone and done it!
Damn! It's clear, she's done it!

I'm jealous. It's no use, I know it's not pretty,
it's disgusting and it's petty.
I'm jealous when I go to the dentist,
when on TV news there's an irredentist,
I'm jealous when we make love, and while asleep
my jealousy becomes deep, so very deep!

I'm afraid everyone knows and my friends eye me with pity,
I try to make you betray yourself through subtle tricks,
I play the liberal in the matter of sex
I stare into your eyes, beg you not to lie,
sulk the whole morning away. One thing I'm sure of,
I'm no longer myself, no longer me, my love!

I'm jealous typing, or maybe worse,
jealous reading Mușina's verse
mad with jealousy when in Kundera everyone sleeps with
all the women, or when Ioana Bulcă steps forth
from the wings with a poem to recite,
I'm jealous when I cut a chunk of Turkish delight.

I'm jealous when I water the flowers, and when I sneeze
suspicion chokes me until I wheeze,
scenarios drive me mad, such a farce,
possibilities, probabilities make me curse,
I'm jealous while I eat or bite a fingernail,
while I fidget or cry and wail…

My love, I'm sorry
this is the story.

[A.J.S./R.S.]

Winter Sunlight

    winter sunlight setting the kitchen curtains ablaze
    God, the crystalline blue sky looks so beautiful
    but I'm old
    and weary.
    I lie right here. and I reflect on my youth.
    my youth is spent. outside, in the white snow—brilliant white—
    sparrows chirp the very same way
    they were heard by Sei Shōnagon
    or Bilitis.

    winter sunlight: Cri.
    "morning moon calls me."
    I've had my… how to express it?…
    when clouds had a nervous system (at least in my poems) and we were
            happy, in spite of the oppression.
    or much earlier: I used to roll film around my fingers
    and then stretch it into small telescopes
    look at us, we've got black-and-white film fingers!
    or even much earlier—when…

    sunlight, winter sunlight! what's become of the recordings we made
    that Christmas? I in one recording room studio
    you in the other, and at a certain moment I said,
    "may life give you" instead of "may God," and we burst into laughter,
    our laughter, then, when we were young
    broke up on the brown magnetic tape—
    now I'm old
    and my name isn't preserved in literary history.

Cri: you're getting older too.
at any moment I'm going to start to bawl.
I'm going to start to tell you: Cri, you were my life, for you
I abandoned the light of my eye.
why can I still remember our first years? we'd brew tea
on the hot metal base of the iron.
we'd make flowers of one-*leu* coins on the shiny surface of the table. otherwise
I remember nothing…
I'd give you a piggyback ride to bed… we'd hop like mad
on Locomotive GT…

winter sunlight, translucent air, clouds without a nervous system,
the sky blue as an orange
as someone once said.
I used to believe I had it in my power to be the universe.
I'd look at my fingers: underneath my wedding-ring
the skin was white, kind of flaking off. I cheated my lawful misery
by means of you, Cri.
then my hair turned gray.
I was covered with psoriasis. the air became full
of the friends' faces. but I had only you, Cri,
as my true friend.
I don't know how to thank you
for allowing me to—

such obscene, wicked premeditation! not a single sincere thought comes to me.
all is effect. my skin raw with patches
my hair gray…
but once I had youth: a hundred thirty pounds of young matter…
nice boobs… but no, no,
I was a man… and yet…
hip-length golden hair…

[A.J.S./D.M.]

I Walk down Water Lily Street in the Bright Sun

On Water Lily Street, next to the cathedral
the light holds us all in its lap
it's a tropical June in '89, with stormy nights and sunny mornings…
I'm meandering, a flâneur
a wedding ring on my finger and my hands in my pockets
it's June '89 and soon this will all be history…
in front of the Student Clinic I catch the stench of hot tar
and right there, asphalt is being laid down, there's a simpatico pair of
        squarish little trucks, yellow and black, pouring out asphalt
I stare at them and wish I had one
I imagine myself at the wheel
in a strawberry-red shirt
I'd spend my life pouring asphalt on the streets…
it's June '89 and the sun's getting lower—

I'd been at the Romanian Book Publishing House, chatting with friends
all the way I kept ogling women and girls
black tights under blue-denim skirts
their cheeks made up, fireproof…

I passed the Muzica shop where
a guy was selling upbeat music out front:
for two bills and a half you could buy a Prince
(he even has pajamas made of denim)
the guy also had, whoa!
for only one and a half, my dear Beatles, "A Hard Day's Night"
(a Russian disk)
I pay
and take the blue LP with me
Electronica and Tehnoton stereo racks gleam in the display windows…

I'm carefree and happy
it's a tropical June in '89
I hang around the trucks pouring asphalt, they spread layer over layer
tar and gravel, so aromatic
I've nothing to do, I stroll like a tourist, like a stranger
my life…
but my life ended long ago…

[A.J.S./D.M.]

A Sudden Autumn, August 30, 1989

at home, I found the bedroom window broken
the cactus on the balcony knocked over, its flower lost
the screen door's mesh damp and torn
outside the wind slammed between buildings
across the street were some guys in undershirts
drinking and laughing in the yellow rectangle of a window
a gust with raindrops
for a few seconds I lingered on the balcony, grabbing the laundry
then I entered my apartment and put on Eddy Grant

I pressed my face against the windowpane, as in my adolescence
I surveyed everything I could see: a gray apartment building with wet streaks
the collective antennas swaying in the wind
nothing more.
I felt lonely; I wished I had a woman
with whom I'd stay in the half-dark
I'd smell her perfume
I'd see the whites of her eyes gleam as it turned dark

then I'd taste her lipstick
the softness of her earlobe...

not a sound, not a movement in the apartment
I hit the power button of the TV on the dressing table
stretched out on the bed
and watched a real broad, a kind of a forewoman
with her hair coiffed,
just the picture, without sound.
Eddy Grant finished what he had to say, too
but I didn't shut off the record player

I fell asleep like this
after the cheetah had sung his hymn
and my sleep was watched over by the gray lice on the TV screen,
the soft spinning of the turntable,
I dreamed I was back with a former girlfriend of mine,
caressing her hair...

[A.J.S./D.M.]

The Occident

the West put my tail between my legs.
I've seen New York and Paris, San Francisco and Frankfurt
I've been where I never dreamt I'd go.
I came home with a stack of photos
and death in my soul.
I'd supposed I meant something, my life meant something.
I'd glimpsed God's eye observing me through the microscope
as I wriggled on the slide.
now I believe in nothing.
I was good enough for a mindless stability
for a bottomless oblivion
for a lonely vagina.
I used to stroll through places that no longer exist now.
oh, my world no longer exists!
my world no longer exists!
my sordid world where I meant something.
I, mircea cărtărescu, am nobody in this new world
there are 1038 mircea cărtărescus here
and people 1038 times better
there are books better than everything I've already written
and women who couldn't care less about them.
the pragmatic egg cracks open and God is present
in his very creation, a pretty-boy God dressed to kill
in magnificent cities and gorgeous autumns
and a sort of sweet southern-Virginia nostalgia in Dorin's
car (country music from the speakers)…

I know my place now
and I know literature's place
for I've seen the Sears Tower
and I've seen Chicago from the top in a greenish fog
while a pair of greyhounds kept running around the terrace of a skyscraper
I told Gabriela as we sat there drinking our Cokes
that my life was at an end.
it's as with Eliot's Magi: I've seen the Occident
I flew over Manhattan
and stared wide-eyed at my spell-struck death.
for this is my *death*.
I stared at display windows with Suzuki motorcycles
and saw myself reflected, dirty, anonymous.
I walked along Königstrasse for hours and hours
among the kids on skateboards.
I was the black-and-white man in a color photograph
Kafka among the Arcadians.
poems, *pohems*, loveangelism
modernisms and bar blab about who's the greatest
halls of fame in a train (returning from Onești): the best
Romanian novels of today
the top ten living poets
just like the Papuans
who still spit in the kettle to make the palm wine ferment…
but poetry is a sign of underdevelopment
and so is staring eye to eye with your God
though you've never actually seen him…

I saw computer games and bookstores—both looked the same to me
I suddenly understood that philosophy is entertainment
that mysticism is showbiz
that here everything is pure surface
but more complex than any depth.
what could I become there? a man bemused, gone batty with happiness
but with his life over.
with his life totally fucked, like the worm in a cherry
who thought himself a big shot
until he woke up in the light, his own filth around him
(my filth, my insufferable poems).
I've seen people for whom abortion law
is more important than the collapse of the Soviets.
I've seen high skies of blue filled with the lights of airplanes
and I've known the roar of four thousand universities.
I've climbed the steps to the top of the Eiffel Tower
I've gone to the top of the Centre Pompidou through the Plexiglas tube
and in Iowa City I've been to the Fox Head…

I've chatted about modernism at Ludwigsburg
with Hassan and Bradbury and Gass and Barth and Federman
the banter of the condemned with his executioner
on my microcassette recorder I caught the swish of the axe
that's going to sever my head from my body.
I felt like sobbing in the luxury of Monrepos:
how is it possible? why were we born to so little purpose?
why should we battle our right-wingers Vadim and Funar?
why for once can't we simply *live*?
why now when at last we can live
do we again breathe the foul stench of garbage bins?
postmodernism and '48-ism

deconstruction and tribalism
pragmatism and navel gazing
with life so dreamlike…

I've seen San Francisco, the blue harbor with ships
and farther out the ocean with forested islands.
the Pacific, can you imagine that!
I dipped my hands in the Pacific "thanking the Lord
for my fingers."
I felt a longing to take leave of my wits.
and in Ferlinghetti's famous bookstore (it does exist!)
it was as if
in a waking dream or a book…
I went gaga over San Francisco's freeways
and Grant Street with so many Chinese tchotchkes
and towering palm trees and the really hilarious
girls in the hair salons
(customers
watched themselves not in mirrors but in color monitors),
and American nights—remember, Mircea T.?
near your house and Melissa's, after
a long afternoon of watching sci-fi movies, eating tacos
and drinking Old Style beer
when we went out and the stars overwhelmed us
the planes floated noiselessly through them
and in your car, an old Ford with frigid air,
you took me across the deserted city to my homey
Mayflower Residence Hall.
and the Thanksgiving and Halloween Parades
with old bankers dressed as bears and clowns
the Czech boy who was hooked on Faulkner

and the small Korean girl in the yellow Cambus
and the melancholy of yellow leaves in Iowa City
and the two of us, Gabi and me, shopping for hours
in Target, K-Mart, Goodwill
and in the fantastic mall downtown…

…I chewed cinnamon candies my first morning in Washington
a camera dangling from my neck in the bitter cold of Dupont Circle…
…I paid $7 to see the New Orleans Zoo
but it was raining and the animals all stayed in their dens…
…in the taxi arguing with the black driver,
not getting a word of what he was saying: "Hey, man…"
…wonderful meals in Chinese and Thai restaurants
and the most wonderful at Meandros, the Greek joint in Soho…
…the Art Institute (impressionists galore)
…the Frick Collection (amazing: three Vermeers!)
…the National Gallery (a Malevich retrospective).

a man frozen for a hundred years
opens his eyes and chooses to die.
what he saw was too beautiful and too sad.
for he had no one there and his infected fingers oozed with panaritium
his teeth were rotten
his mind held
all sorts of useless things
and everything he'd ever done
half-seemed written on wind.
a man on a faraway island invented
a sewing machine of bamboo
and thought himself a genius, for no one in his tribe
had ever made anything like that. when the Dutch arrived

they rewarded him for his invention
and gave him the electric version instead.
(thank you, he said, and chose to die).
I no longer can find a place for myself anywhere, I no longer belong here
and cannot belong there either.

and what about poetry? I feel like the last Mohican
as ridiculous as Denver the Dinosaur.
the best poetry is tolerable poetry,
nothing else: merely tolerable.
we made good poetry for ten years
without an inkling of how stupid our poetry was.
we made great literature, and now it dawns on us
that it cannot cross the threshold, precisely because it's big,
grand, stifled by flab.
this poem isn't poetry either
for only what is *not* poetry
can endure as poetry
only what *cannot* be poetry.

the West opened my eyes but knocked my head against the lintel
and brought me down low.
I leave to others my life until today.
let others believe in what I believed.
let others love what I loved.
I no longer can.
no longer can. no longer can.

[A.J.S./B.Ş.]

August 14 (Listening to "Woman")

smile at me and I haven't a care in the world
I don't want anything else
I don't want the Nobel or to write another line
I don't want to live forever
I don't want to be the world's miracle
I want only you, only you!

tell me again that you're mine
let me know you'll always be mine alone
oh, God, spare me this pain
this craziness
this fear!

laugh with me again, just say my name
press your face to my face, be mine,
be mine, be mine!
I don't want music, friends or other chicks
I don't want to go live in the U.S.A.
I don't want to be far away from you,
from you, from you!

put your little hand in mine and let's take a walk
to the Romanian Book and the Writers' Union
let's browse in antique stores, let's wander the streets
stay in the kitchen with me
don't forget, Cri, my life's in your hands!

[A.J.S./R.S.]

Nothing

fuck depression!
I've had it with begging for compassion!
with being in charge of the Union's operation!
with always being nagged, "hurry, write! hurry, orate!"
concentrate, you s.o.b.!
create, create, create!
davai, davai! don't stop! a novel a year till you drop!
get yourself in gear and keep it up,
to remain among the living here,
to make a place for sure in the history of literature!
to be worthy of our culture!

I've had it with feeling bad after I've written!
with feeling bad after I've not written!
with your staring at me as if I were the walking dead
whenever I haven't spewed forth pages or read!
maybe my brain's sick and tired
of you; of everything and everybody—all this shit!
it's possible I've glimpsed your sagging tit
when I lit the lamp in the bedroom,
your rhymestress's literary fit!

it's too much! it's driven me mad!
my brain's fallen apart, gone bad,
the God who used to provide light and an answer
lately has contracted esophageal cancer.
I don't want to cross that threshold!

I've written poetry for fifteen years
and today everyone sneers and jeers,
literature's illiterates, ill-willed scribblers,
once friends, now pissers, ass-kissers!

davai, davai! you wouldn't give a damn if I just upchuck!
cărtărescu's plumb out of luck!
we're rescued from an obsession!
may he rest in peace!
it's his fault we couldn't recover from our disaster!
third-rate poetaster!
in his latest book at long last it's obvious

that all this time he's been worthless beyond repair!
a bicycle pump has puffed him up with air!

                …and perhaps it's true…
                …the devil knows, perhaps it's true…

anyhow, I want you to know that I don't give two *sous*.
I no longer peek at my reviews
I don't visit anyone to gossip about news
I won't write even a letter.
I am truly at peace!
my life hasn't ceased and I feel much better.

                                        [A.J.S./D.M.]

MIRCEA CĂRTĂRESCU is Romania's most celebrated writer from the highly accomplished group of self-consciously postmodernist writers who began to publish in the 1980s—the "blue-jeans generation," one strongly influenced by American examples. His first book of poetry, *Headlights, Shop Windows, Photographs*, appeared in 1980. Other titles include *Love Poems* (1982); *Everything* (1984); *Nothing* (2010); *The Levant* (1990); *Love* (1994); a collection of love poems, *Double CD* (1998); *Fifty Sonnets* (2003); and the collected two-volume *Pluriverse* (2003). Adam J. Sorkin's co-translations of Cărtărescu's poetry in collaborative versions have appeared in *Another Chicago Magazine, Poetry New York, Exquisite Corpse, New Delta Review, Talisman, Poetry Wales, Parthenon West, Modern Poetry in Translation, Ping-Pong, Cutthroat, Saranac Review, Lana Turner, Connotation Press, Glint* and *Poem* [in the UK], as well as the anthologies *Leading Contemporary Poets, Speaking the Silence, Born in Utopia* and *Bucharest Tales*. A group of fourteen of the poems came out as *Bebop Baby* in the *Poetry New York* chapbook series in 1999.

In the early 1990s, after the fall of communism and the end of censorship, Cărtărescu turned exclusively to prose. He has published more than fifteen volumes of fiction and essays. His novel *Nostalgia* (translated by Julian Semilian) was published by New Directions in 1989; University of Plymouth Press published his book of stories and essays, *Why We Love Women* (translated by Alistair Ian Blyth), in 2011; the English version of the first book of his *Blinding: Book One* trilogy *(Orbitor)*, translated by Sean Cotter, was published by Archipelago Books in 2013. Cărtărescu's literary recognitions include numbers of awards and prizes from the Romanian Writers' Union and the Association of Professional Writers of Romania (ASPRO); the Romanian Academy Prize; the Vilenica Prize; the Spycher – Literary Prize Leuk, Switzerland; the Leipzig Book Award for European Understanding; the Austrian State Prize for European Literature; and the Premio Gregor von Rezzori, these latter all for *Blinding* in various translations. In 2018, he was awarded the Prix Formentor and the Thomas Mann Prizes and in 2019 the Prix Millepages and Prix Transfuge for his most recent novel, *Solenoid*, among many accolades celebrating his achievement. *Solenoid* is being translated by Sean Cotter.

Mircea Cărtărescu, whose work has appeared in sixteen European languages and Japanese besides English, has also been Romania's Nobel Prize nominee. He is professor at the Faculty of Letters of the University of Bucharest.

Translators

ADAM J. SORKIN has published more than sixty books of Romanian poetry in translation and his work has won the 2005 Poetry Society (UK) Prize for European Poetry Translation as well as the *International Quarterly* Crossing Boundaries, Kenneth Rexroth, Ioan Flora Poetry Translation, and Poesis Translation Prizes, among others. He has been awarded Fulbright, Rockefeller Foundation, Arts Council of England, New York State Arts Council, Academy of American Poets, Soros Foundation, Romanian Cultural Institute, and US National Endowment for the Arts support for his literary activity.

Among his recent books (all with co-translators) are *The Hunchbacks' Bus* by Nora Iuga (Bitter Oleander Press, 2016, longlisted for the 2017 National Translation Award in Poetry); *Syllables of Flesh*, poems by Floarea Țuțuianu (Plamen Press, 2017, with illustrations by Țuțuianu); and *A Deafening Silence*, poems by Magda Cârneci (Shearsman Books, also 2017). In 2018, Sorkin published Mircea Dinescu's *The Barbarians' Return* (Bloodaxe Books), and a group of his translations together with Diana Manole of the poetry of the major Moldovan author Emilian Galaicu-Păun earned second prize in the John Dryden Translation Competition (UK). In 2020, Sorkin published Ioana Ieronim's *Lavinia and Her Daughters*, translated with the poet (Somerville, MA: Červená Barva Press), and Aura Christi's *The God's Orbit*, translated with Petru Iamandi (Wivenhoe, Colchester, Essex [UK]: Mica Press) is forthcoming in October.

Adam J. Sorkin is Distinguished Professor of English Emeritus, Penn State Brandywine.

Co-Translators

ILEANA CIOCÂRLIE is Senior Research Fellow/Associate Professor at "G. Călinescu" Institute for Literary History and Theory, Romanian Academy, Bucharest, is co-author of Dicționarul General al Literaturii Române, București, Editura Univers Enciclopedic, 2004-2009.

CRISTINA HANGANU-BRESCH is a graduate of the University of Bucharest, where she attended Mircea Cărtărescu's lectures on Romanian literature as well as his writing circle. Currently, she is Associate Professor of Writing and Rhetoric at the University of the Sciences in Philadelphia.

IOANA IERONIM is a well-known Romanian poet, translator, and playwright. She has translated seven books of her poetry with Adam J. Sorkin including *The Triumph of the Water Witch* (Bloodaxe Books, 2000) and *Lavinia and Her Daughters* (Červená Barva Press, 2020).

DANIEL MANGU graduated with a degree in English from the University of Bucharest and worked as a journalist for Romanian Radio before moving the UK, where he now works in finance.

MIRELA SURDULESCU graduated from the University of Bucharest, the English Department. Apart from teaching English, she has been active in translating from English into Romanian works of poetry and fiction, as well as technical and economic texts.

RADU SURDULESCU is Professor of English and Cultural Anthropology at the University of Bucharest. His publications include books, anthologies and articles in the fields of Critical Theory, Literature and Anthropology, as well as translations of poetry and prose between English and Romanian.

BOGDAN ȘTEFĂNESCU is Professor of English and Vice-Rector of the University of Bucharest, where he teaches British Literature, Nationalism Studies, Comparative Cultural Study of Post/communism and Post/colonialism. He has published literary translations and research on European romanticism, post/communism, post/colonialism, and the discourse of national identity.

MIRCEA CĂRTĂRESCU ON ADAM J. SORKIN:

I was always impressed by Adam Sorkin's devotion to Romanian poetry. To say that he is the best translator of poetry from Romanian into English is to tell only a part of the truth. Actually, he is the reinventor of the Romanian contemporary poetry in the English speaking world. His translations are unique in their fine balance between accuracy and poetic beauty.

—Speaking the Silence, 2001

Made in the USA
Middletown, DE
21 June 2023

33015616R00083